# Dear Kallah

# Dear Kallah

## A Practical Guide for the New Bride

**Malka Kaganoff**

FELDHEIM PUBLISHERS
Jerusalem • New York

The examples in this book are all fictional. Any similarity to real people or situations is purely coincidental.

First published 1993

Copyright © 1993 by Malka Kaganoff
ISBN 0-87306-633-2

**Library of Congress Cataloging-in-Publication Data**

Kaganoff, Malka.
Dear kallah / by Malka Kaganoff.
      p. cm.
      Includes index.
      ISBN 0-87306-633-2. — ISBN 0-87306-634-0 (pocket size)
      1. Women, Jewish—Religious life. 2. Communication in
marriage. I. Title.
BM726,K34 1993
296.7'4—dc20                              93-18123

**Feldheim Publishers**
200 Airport Executive Park
Spring Valley, N.Y. 10977

POB 35002
Jerusalem, Israel

*Printed in Israel*

הרב לוי יצחק הלוי הורוויץ

דער באסטאנער רבי

Grand Rabbi Levi Y. Horowitz

מוסדות בוסטון באה"ק
בנשיאות האדמו"ר שליט"א
מעלות האדמו"ר מבוסטון ו
Israel הר נוף, ירושלים

ב"ה

**25 July 1991**
**15 Av 5751**

The society in which we are living can at times introduce us to thorny problems that may be too much for us to tackle by ourselves. This applies to those contemplating marriage who wish to do so strictly *al taharas ha-kodesh.*

*Dear Kallah* by Mrs. Malka Kaganoff, a manual for *kallahs,* is certainly a valuable addition to the information a *kallah* needs when establishing her home. The examples presented by the author strike home quite often and are representative of the problems we find in many marriages. As the saying goes, "An ounce of prevention is worth a pound of cure." And as *Chazal* tell us, the respect a husband and wife show each other is most critical to preserving *shalom bayis.*

May the *Ribbono shel Olam* grant *hatzlachah* to all who contemplate the most serious new stage in their life — that of building a *bayis ne'eman b'Yisrael.*

Bi'Vrachah,

Grand Rabbi Levi Y. Horowitz
The Bostoner Rebbe

# Acknowledgments

First and foremost I would like to thank *Hashem Yisbarach* for all He has given me, and specifically for the opportunity to teach His Torah.

Many thanks go to members of my family and my friends who read and reread parts of this book for me. Thank you also to the staff of Feldheim Publishers, whose expertise greatly enhanced this book.

I am very grateful to the Bostoner Rebbe, who took the time to review this manuscript and write a recommendation.

I would like to express my appreciation to my parents, Rabbi Dr. and Mrs. Philip Zimmerman, for all they have done for me. It was in their home that I received my initial Torah education, and they have been an ongoing source of support and encouragement for me.

My deepest appreciation goes to my husband, Rabbi Yirmiyohu Kaganoff. Throughout the years he has helped me in many ways, and it is my fervent hope that I am a true *ezer* to him.

This book is dedicated
To my wonderful husband,
Rabbi Yirmiyohu Kaganoff,
with sincere tefillos to Hashem Yisbarach
that our *bayis ne'eman* continues to flourish.

To my children,
Chaya Baila, Shlomo, Dovid Shimon, Sara Leah,
Yaakov, Miriam, and Menachem Nochum.
May Hashem grant us the wisdom
to guide them to maximize their potential
as *ovdei Hashem*;
and may we merit to enjoy *nachas* from them
as they each build a *bayis ne'eman b'Yisrael.*

And to every kallah as she sets out
to build her own *bayis ne'eman.*
To each kallah I wish that
Hashem will grant you success on your life's path.

# Contents

# Dear Kallah:

I saw a *kallah* walking with her *chasan* the other day. There was a bounce to her step and a smile on her lips. The two of them were involved in conversation, and were not focusing on the rest of the world. I could tell that they thought that life was just perfect. Why shouldn't it be? The *kallah* has found her true partner in life, with the help of Hashem's kindness. Their days are full of excitement, planning, and the special relationship that they share. Things are indeed perfect at this point in their lives. They realize that there may be some obstacles, but they feel that there is nothing that the two of them together cannot surmount.

When I saw them, I wanted to walk over to the *kallah* and share some thoughts with her. "You are truly fortunate," I would say. "You will be starting your *bayis ne'eman* (faithful home) on a positive note. Hashem has sent you a fine *chasan*, and you share beautiful goals. Please invest the effort necessary to maintain this *berachah*. Don't neglect your *bayis*. Right now you are putting effort into planning the wedding. Don't forget to plan the marriage, too."

This little book is a collection of thoughts and recommendations that I wish to share with you and all *kallahs*. This book is not all-inclusive; there are many other good books available. Perhaps this book, written directly to you, as a *kallah*, will provide you with some food for thought as you enter this momentous time of your life. May Hashem bless you with success in your goal of creating a *binyan adei ad* (an everlasting edifice).

The recommendations made in the following pages are culled from my many interactions with *kallahs* and married women who I have taught and advised. In addition, I have taken the time to go through many Torah sources on the topic of *shalom bayis*. The results are presented here with concrete examples for clarity.

Throughout this book you will find messages to repeat to yourself. If you are not accustomed to talking to yourself, it is a skill worth learning. People are basically logical, and can often advise others. It is more difficult to give oneself advice since, when an individual is personally involved, feelings can cloud logic. Those individuals who learn to talk calmly to themselves will succeed in putting their feelings into a proper perspective.

An example:

> You perceive that a relative is not speaking in a polite fashion to you. Your automatic reaction is to feel hurt. You stop for a minute and send yourself a message.

Sample message:

People don't always realize how they sound. They often neglect to act politely if something unrelated is bothering them.

This message can have a calming effect and you can begin to look for different interpretations of the relative's manner. Maybe the relative is tired or upset about something. The initial reaction of personal hurt can be redirected to a feeling of sympathy for the other person.

One request: As you begin this book, you might decide that most of the ideas are not so novel. You may feel that you could have thought of them on your own. This may be true, and no claims are made that this book has innovations never seen before. The purpose of this book is to present these ideas in a clear fashion, as an available reference. So please read this book now before you are married, and refer back to it later.

*B'virkas kol tuv,*
Malka Kaganoff

P.S. The stories told in this book actually occurred, or could occur, but the names and details have been changed.

*Chapter One*

*The Beginning*

Dear *Kallah*,

You are now at the very beginning of a wonderful marriage. You have the opportunity to start off properly. It is much easier for a *kallah* to initially learn the right attitudes and interaction skills than to relearn and retrain herself after she has grown accustomed to various nonproductive patterns. There are many factors to consider when entering a marriage. Listed below are a few of these factors.

◆ Commitment

This is your marriage for the rest of your life, God willing, and you are going to invest the effort and make the adjustments necessary to keep it flourishing. Hashem has sent you your life's partner, one who is predestined for you. This partner is the completion of your *neshamah*. Your mission is to maintain *shalom bayis* and build a true *bayis ne'eman*. As time passes, these goals must be remembered and reexamined.

Message 1: Hashem has sent me my life's partner, and I am committed to make our marriage grow.

3

## ◆ Sensitivity

Until marriage, an individual attends to him or herself and works on personal growth. After marriage, another person must be considered at all times. Whereas any *kallah* knows, on an intellectual level, that sensitivity toward her *chasan* is a high priority, conscious effort is necessary to translate this conviction into practice. The *kallah* has to train herself repeatedly to keep a spouse's feelings in mind. Naturally, people seldom *intentionally* do things to hurt their spouses, but many inadvertent slights could be avoided with some thought. A wife can try to anticipate what makes her husband comfortable, even if he doesn't verbalize his feelings.

> Devorah looks forward to a day of shopping with her husband. Her plans include a visit to a favorite aunt of hers. Devorah should take the time to consider how comfortable her husband will be with this plan.

**Message 2: Am I considering my husband's feelings?**

## ◆ Expectations

Everyone walks into marriage with expectations, based upon their upbringing. When expectations are not met, disappointment results. These expectations are often subconscious, and neither the *chasan* nor the *kallah* can identify the root of a disagreement until the underlying expectations are clarified.

> Yehudis has been married for just two weeks. She assumes that her husband will buy the challahs for Shabbos since that is what her father does. Her husband is unaware that she made that assumption. If she greets him *erev Shabbos* at 2 P.M. with "Why didn't you buy the challahs?", he will feel hurt and perplexed. If Yehudis wants her husband to assume the responsibility of buying challahs and tells him politely, he probably will be very agreeable to do so.

The above example of challahs is rather simple and easy to rectify. People come into marriage with many varied expectations, and are disappointed when these expectations are not met. One woman may expect her husband to be her learning partner, another might expect her husband to sit and converse with her for two hours every night. Analysis of expectations is the first step to establishing mutually acceptable routines. (Communication and compromise are the next steps. See chapter 2.) Sometimes people set up unrealistic expectations, and their happiness depends on their ability to discard those demands. People date with imaginary mental lists of what they expect to find in a mate. A wise *kallah* puts her list aside as soon as she becomes engaged.

Message 3: Am I reacting on the basis of my unwritten assumptions? Did I clarify all my expectations with my husband?

◆ Creating an island — with bridges
Right after your wedding, there is a new household in existence. It is similar to an island with bridges. A couple interacts with the rest of the world, but at the same time maintains seclusion and privacy.

*1. Relatives*
There are many well-meaning relatives who wish to be involved in the life of a newly married couple. Indeed, their interest is appreciated, and they can be very supportive, but the couple must create an independent life that revolves around the two of them exclusively. Although a girl may have a close relationship with her mother, after marriage certain issues must be left on this private island.

Parents do make assumptions and requests. These requests should be assessed by the husband and wife together, so that decisions that are mutually acceptable will be reached.

> Yaffa's parents expect her and her husband, Asher, to visit them every Sunday. Yaffa loves her parents, but she realizes that this schedule is not practical. She and Asher sit down to discuss the situation and decide that they will visit every other week, and call twice a week. Although Yaffa wishes that she could comply with her parents' request, she understands that her main focus should be on building her home with Asher.

Although a husband and wife should envision themselves on their private island, they need not imagine that they are isolated. Extended families provide a beautiful support system to a newly married couple. In addition, at times it is very helpful and proper to reach out for guidance to a *Rav* or mentor on any number of matters. The *Rav* can steer a couple in the right direction. Occasionally, adherence to certain *halachos* will cause strain in a relationship. A *Rav* must be consulted. The *halachah* cannot be changed, of course, but a *Rav* will have the expertise to guide a couple in how to integrate the *halachos* into the situation at hand in the most appropriate manner.

*2. Friends*
Good friends are very important, and it is not necessary to distance yourself from them after your wedding. However, discretion is necessary when deciding which topics you will not discuss with others. Also remember, if you tell people negative things about your marriage, they will be remembered by others long after they have been forgotten by you.

*3. Other men*
As this island is fortified, a woman's relationship with men other than her husband is curtailed (with the exception of close family members).

*4. Concerns about the opinion of others*
It is proper to act in a way that will create a positive impression on friends and relatives. However, the major

consideration when making a decision is *what is best for our island and our home* and not what others will think.

> Sara, a young *kallah*, is perfectly content to forgo a dining room set so that the money can be used elsewhere. But she wonders what her friends and relatives will think. Concentrate on your island, Sara!

Message 4: Am I creating a proper balance between independence and good relationships with others?

◆ Every husband is unique — avoid comparisons

People are constantly making comparisons. Little children stand back-to-back to see who is taller. It takes a conscious effort to outgrow the urge to compare yourself and your family to others. Comparison of your husband to someone else's husband is unproductive and is to be avoided at all times. Just as it does not matter if one husband is taller than another husband, other comparisons are also irrelevant.

There are two reasons why it is unwise to compare. Firstly, one cannot be sure what someone else's husband is really like. A friend's husband may seem kind or helpful, whereas the facts could be very different. Secondly, no two people can be compared. People possess so many qualities; one person has one strength and another has a different one. No person is in the position to decide who is better and who is worse.

> Adina wants her husband to take her on a vacation. Will this question motivate him to do it: "Why can't you take me on a vacation like Shani's husband does?"

The following message should be repeated whenever one starts to make mental comparisons.

Message 5: Comparisons are unproductive.

◆ Appreciating differences

Hashem, in His infinite wisdom, made men and women different from each other in many ways. It is important for a woman to be aware of these differences so that she can better understand her husband. Women tend to be more verbal, more sensitive and more emotional than men. They are more intuitive and more attentive to physical details than their husbands. Not all women fit these generalizations, but it is valuable for both husband and wife to take the time to understand their spouse's nature.

> Chava and Moshe went to pick out a wedding band. Moshe's parents had recommended one specific store, which was owned by friends of theirs. Chava could not decide which ring she liked best and sat deliberating for a long time. Moshe couldn't comprehend why someone had to be so particular about a ring, and he began to pressure Chava to make her choice quickly. Moshe did not appreciate that jewelry is important to most women, and that Chava was determined to put much thought into the choice of a ring. If he had realized that Chava was not being unreasonable, he would have been more understanding. If Chava had realized that, as a man, Moshe could not be expected automatically to understand how important this was to her, she might not have felt hurt by his lack of sensitivity and rushing her.

If a husband seems baffled by his wife's nature, the wife should not respond with an attempt to give up her femininity. A man wants to be married to a woman who has feminine characteristics, not to one who acts like a male colleague.

There can be many differences between two spouses, based on each one's background and upbringing. What is acceptable in one family may not be acceptable in another. The ability to recognize and accept these differences is important in making a smooth adjustment. Also, the way people go about doing things often cannot be labeled as *right* or *wrong*, but people are more comfortable with the patterns familiar to them.

> Etti's family has always been very health-conscious. Hot dogs and lunch meats have never been on the menu. Yitzchak is accustomed to those foods, and does not feel a need to modify his diet when he marries Etti. Yitzchak should resist the urge to mock Etti for her adherence to this healthful regimen. Etti, too, should be careful not to ridicule Yitzchak for his habits. Although she may wish to convince Yitzchak of the benefits of her eating habits, she should not mount an aggressive campaign to reform him. Hopefully, if Etti gradually introduces alternative food choices without belittling Yitzchak, changes will occur over a period of time.

Still other differences can be attributed to one's personality and temperament. One person will leave everything to the last minute; another will be ready far in advance. One person will enjoy spending *Yom Tov* at home; another will enjoy going to relatives. The list is endless. In all cases, equitable compromises can be achieved if both partners begin with the attitude of accepting their spouse's differences.

> Ahuva got sick shortly after her wedding. Her husband Michael politely inquired if she needed anything. He brought her Kleenex and tea, and then left her alone for several hours. Ahuva was perplexed and hurt. She would have appreciated her husband's company. Why did he disappear? Ahuva recovered after a day or two, and she chose not to bring up Michael's so-called strange behavior.
>
> Several months later, Michael didn't feel well. Ahuva attended to his needs and then pulled up a chair to keep him company. She wanted to demonstrate how to attend a sick spouse. Ahuva was further perplexed when Michael requested that she leave him alone. It took her a while to realize that, although she appreciated company when she was ill, her husband preferred peace and quiet.

### ◆ Honesty and trust

A marriage must be based on trust. People who trust one another have a positive feeling toward each other. If someone feels that he has been deceived, he will find it hard to maintain his trust. Once trust has been broken, it is difficult to reestablish it. It is simpler to begin with a commitment to honesty. Honesty does not imply that a person must disclose every derogatory thought that crosses his mind. Discretion is necessary to decide which things are better left unsaid, but what is said should be the truth.

> Tova had just turned twenty. Her parents told the *shadchan* that she was nineteen, so the *shadchan* told Meir that Tova was nineteen. Several months later Tova and Meir became engaged. Tova felt that the time had come to tell Meir her real age, but she couldn't bring herself to do so. What an uncomfortable feeling for a young *kallah*, to enter marriage with some measure of dishonesty! And when Meir eventually discovers the discrepancy on his own, will he not feel that his trust has been misplaced?

An underlying theme in this book is that marriage requires effort. This is a concept that some find difficult to fully comprehend because the society we live in is devoted to making everything in life as effortless as possible. It also leads us to expect instant results. Consider the calculator, the microwave and the computer; these are just a few of the inventions that discourage effort and encourage us to expect results immediately.

In addition to not recognizing the value of effort, a young person is influenced by today's society to consider many things in life as disposable. After all, we throw out paper plates, aluminum baking pans and broken tape recorders.

Previous generations were taught the value of repairing an item when necessary in order to make it serviceable as new. Today it is far more expedient to replace the item. So in essence, we are not accustomed to preserving things.

Since we subconsciously treat many things as disposable, it is important to stress that there are certain things in life that are too precious to throw out. Greater effort is required to maintain something than to discard it, and as we said, we live in a society where effort is also discouraged, so we must be careful not to be lulled into underestimating the need for effort in many situations. You should always keep your marriage foremost in your mind as something permanent and valuable, something certainly worth the investment of constant effort in order to improve it. Results may not be instantaneous, but the rewards will be great.

*Chapter Two*
## Improving a Perfect Marriage

After entering a marriage with a positive attitude, thought still must be invested on ways to keep the marriage growing. Let us picture a strong marriage — a healthy relationship where love is ever-growing. The couple blessed with this type of marriage still can benefit from some of the recommendations in this chapter.

◆ Appreciation

Taking others for granted is a common human failing. We rarely thank our parents properly, and we never properly thank our Creator. There are many reasons for this. The more familiar we are with certain people, the less we appreciate them. In addition, people like to feel independent. When we express appreciation, we are admitting that we benefited from the help of someone else. In marriage, it is important to acknowledge the *interdependence* of husband and wife.

On a concrete level, a thank-you is in order whenever your husband does something considerate or helpful. On a deeper level, however, you should also feel a sense of appreciation at these times. If you do not assume that your husband owes you anything, you will appreciate more all the things he gives.

> Esther, a young *kallah*, recently told me that she and her *chasan* were driving somewhere. She pointed out the exit they needed to her *chasan* and he expressed his appreciation for her assistance with a large thank-you. "It made me feel like a million dollars," Esther concluded.

**Message 8: Do I remember to say "thank you"? Do I appreciate my husband for what he is and what he does?**

*Note:* At this point you may be thinking that not only the wife has to keep these factors in mind. Shouldn't these also be the husband's considerations? Yes. That is certainly correct. Husbands, too, have to put great effort into establishing and maintaining their *bayis ne'eman*. They have to learn communication skills and develop a sensitivity toward their wives. This book, however, is addressed to *kallah*s. It is much easier for a husband to act properly toward a helpful wife than toward one who is not. If both husband and wife concentrate on their own personal obligations, true harmony will result.

◆ Ezer k'negdo

The Torah characterizes a wife as a helpmate (*ezer*). Women are noted for their involvement in *chesed* projects. As soon as a *kallah* gets married, she has a person in the house whom she can assist; someone for whom she can continually perform *chesed*. A good wife does what her husband wants, and endeavors to make his life more pleasant. She respects his opinions and regards him as the captain of their ship. However, the wife is endowed with *binah yeserah* (additional understanding), and she is able to set the atmosphere aboard this ship.

> One of the most beautiful testimonials to a supportive wife is a plaque on a wall of Yeshivas Ner Yisrael of Baltimore.

It is a memorial to the late Rebbitzen Ruderman ע״ה, on which the words of Rabbi Akiva are used to praise her. "That which is mine and that which is yours is hers."

The second half of this phrase, *k'negdo* (opposite him), can be interpreted to mean "reflecting him." One of the roles of a wife is to provide corrective criticism and feedback. It is very difficult to see oneself objectively. A wife can be a mirror of truth for her husband. Of course tact is required, and the husband must first receive the message that his wife has his best interests in mind. It is important that the husband not feel that his wife is critical of him. If the husband feels that his wife has truly placed him as the head of the house, he will be more willing to accept her input.

Benny finds it hard to get out in the evening to go to a *shiur*. Sima realizes that her husband isn't perfect, and that she must respect him for all the good things he is and does. In this instance, she has the opportunity to be a *k'negdo* with positive results. If she mutters snide remarks how her brothers always manage to go to *shiurim* at night, she will not accomplish anything. If she doesn't say anything but looks down at Benny, he will soon feel it. However, if Sima analyzes the problem and decides to act wisely, she can be a positive influence. She can try to organize the household so that Benny can leave punctually. She can make sure to greet him pleasantly when he returns, and let him know how much she respects his efforts to learn. Hopefully, Benny will meet her assessment of him as one who is motivated to learn, even at night. Sima must keep in mind that change is difficult and she should not become too frustrated if success is not immediate.

A wife who provides encouragement, guidance, and support can help her husband grow to reach his full potential.

[*Note:* If the situation in the above story is different, and Sima finds it difficult to do without Benny's presence in the evening, communication and discussion are necessary to arrive at a workable arrangement that will benefit the whole household.]

Message 9: What can I do to make my husband's life easier? Am I being a true *ezer k'negdo*?

◆ Communication and compromise

Communication is basic to a marriage. If a wife is upset about a particular situation and does not tell her husband, how will he know? The husband may be a wise man, but he is not a prophet. Feelings must be communicated. When discussing matters, disagreements will often arise. It is unreasonable to assume that spouses will always automatically agree on everything. A pleasant discussion can be very productive and can lead to compromises that both sides can live with. In most cases compromises can be reached. If not, a wife should be careful not to dismiss her husband's wishes. If she feels that her husband's requests run counter to *halachah*, then she should seek the advice of a *Rav*.

The attitude with which both partners enter a discussion is vital. The goal of a discussion is that husband and wife together address a situation, not that the husband and his opinion clash with the wife and her opinion.

> Dina told me that she asks her husband, "Are you in a good mood?" If he says yes, she says, "Good! So let's have our fight now." Dina realizes that some controversial matters have to be discussed. The wise thing to do is to bring them up when she and her husband can discuss them pleasantly.

> Shira wanted to go to a restaurant for her anniversary. She didn't mention anything to her husband, David, hoping that he would realize what she wanted on his own. Shira was very hurt that David did not fulfill her wish, and celebrated their anniversary at home. Is he at fault for not being a mind reader?

### ◆ Attentiveness

You know that you feel gratified when someone greets you with a cheery hello. Likewise you have the opportunity to brighten your husband's day whenever you greet him. There are many ways to make your husband feel that you care about him. If your husband states an opinion, let him know that you value it. If he voices a preference for a certain outfit or food, respect his wishes. If a wife is chatting on the phone when her husband comes home, she would be wise to end the conversation and focus her attention on her husband. Some women change into informal clothes as soon as they come home. Care must be taken to assure that a wife never looks unkempt to her husband.

A husband is to be complimented sincerely. Although a wife might feel proud of her husband's accomplishments, if she does not verbalize it, he will not know it. It is a common fallacy to assume that spouses do not need to express their feelings to each other. Silence can easily be misinterpreted.

A wife may be very busy and put much energy into many projects. But imagine how a husband feels if his wife is exhausted whenever he comes home in the evening. A mother of small children should try to find a way to catch up on needed sleep during the daytime, and not be exhausted when her husband comes home. Tiredness is not conducive to *shalom bayis*, since it can lead to irritability. In addition, if a wife is perpetually tired for her husband, he may get the message that he is not very important to her.

Although it is good to pay attention to a husband, it is also necessary to give him the space he requires. If he does not want to share his feelings at that moment, his need for solitude should be respected without interruption. A man who feels important in his home, and feels that his wife believes in him and understands him, will maximize his potential and accomplish more than a man who does not feel this way.

Message 11: I have to make sure that I don't inadvertently ignore my husband and his preferences.

*Chapter Three*
# *Reaching toward Your Goal*

You have started on the right track (chapter 1) and thought about putting effort into your marriage (chapter 2). With Hashem's help you are now on your way to a strong marriage and a vibrant *bayis ne'eman.* Such a relationship is truly beautiful. Husband and wife can assist each other and make each other's life more comfortable. They can be sensitive to each other's needs, and choose what is best for the two of them as a unit. Marriage provides an environment where love can grow. Hashem has sent these two people to each other, and they have grown together.

## ◆ 1+1=1

The ultimate goal of marriage is to unite two individuals into one unit. Both husband and wife learn to think of *us* rather than *me* and *you.*

> Reb Aryeh Levin, the famous giant of *chesed*, accompanied his wife to the doctor. He proceeded to explain the nature of the problem. "Doctor, my wife's foot is hurting *us.*"

It is helpful to remember that we are not all Reb Aryeh Levin, and that this is a level that takes years to achieve. However, if one sets his or her sights on this goal, it can be achieved to a large extent. It requires training to think about *us* instead of about *me*, but the goal is to adapt and always keep in mind the following formula:

$$1(me) + 1(he) = 1(we)$$

There are two major factors that make this equation so difficult to work out as it should. Each partner enters marriage from a different background, with an independent personality. This alone makes adapting difficult. It is compounded by the influences of a society which encourages selfishness and attending to one's own needs as a priority. The Torah, too, advocates attending to Number One, but Number One in a Torah perspective is the couple, not the individual.

Message 12: A marriage involves focusing on *us* more than on *me*.

#### ◆ Love and affection

The Rambam, in his *Mishneh Torah*, records the obligation of a man to love his wife. There are two things that can be learned from this. First, although the media has debased and exploited love, it is indeed a Jewish concept and an integral part of a marriage. Second, since love has been commanded, it must be a goal that one can work toward. Although love is an emotion, people do not have to sit and wait to "fall in love." Love grows between a couple when it is properly nurtured. True love is experienced after marriage. As a couple works together at common goals, the love between them increases.

Rav Dessler points out that the word *ahavah* (love) comes from the word *hav*, which means "to give." This is the main method of strengthening love. The more you give to someone, the more you love that person. In addition, care should be taken to create a feeling of closeness between the partners and not to create barriers. Both partners can

take care to behave in a manner that will make it easier for
their spouses to love them.

Although the dictates of *tzenius* limit public demon-
stration of affection between spouses, private verbal and
physical gestures of affection are within the Torah frame-
work. A note, a gift, or just a smile can go a long way to
help a couple grow together.

**Message 13: What am I doing to nurture the love between us?**

◆ A very private discussion

The guidelines of *tzenius* and modesty deem it inappropriate to discuss here the physical relationship between a
husband and wife. I will mention but a few concepts relating to this topic, and then encourage all *kallah*s to inquire
about the Torah perspective of a physical relationship from
a woman who is competent to present such a viewpoint.

Since Hashem set up the relationship between a husband and wife to include a physical relationship, it is un-
derstood that this is an integral positive aspect of relating
and is not in any way embarrassing. It is intensely private,
and covered by a veil of secrecy. Just as in any other aspect
of marriage, a couple must grow together in this area too.
There is one concept that is valuable to keep in mind.
Each partner should ask him/herself the following question: "What can I do to further our relationship and make
my spouse's life more enjoyable and meaningful?" This
conscientious attempt to focus on making your partner
happy will reap great benefits.

**Message 14: Am I viewing the physical relationship in marriage
in its true Torah perspective?**

◆ Help from Above

We daven for so many things in life; we should include
in our prayers requests for a strong, loving relationship
and a pleasant marriage. One *tefillah* which some women

say before they use the *mikveh* requests the following: "Hashem, please make sure that my husband has eyes for me only."* Any personal prayer can be added in which you can pray to have the qualities of a good wife, such as wisdom and patience. After you have done your best to act in a supportive manner, and you have prayed to Hashem for His assistance, you can relax, knowing that you have turned to the One Who can and does provide.

*Printed in *Chuppas Chasanim.*

## Chapter Four
## Maintaining a Newness

As a *kallah*, your relationship with your *chasan* is one of the most important parts of your life. There are many issues that you wish to discuss as you begin to build a relationship of caring and affection. At this point in your life, it is difficult to imagine that people need to be *told* to make time in their lives for their spouses. This chapter and those that follow may not seem applicable right now, but please read them through and have them available for future reference.

Although we have said that love grows over time, there is something special about the excitement of the new relationship between an engaged couple. The goal is to maintain the freshness of the relationship as time goes on.

◆ Share your days

Life speeds by at a hectic pace. Husbands and wives follow independent schedules. These schedules usually intersect for brief moments, and then spin off in different directions. One simple suggestion to help married people grow together, and not apart, is for them to tell each other what they have done that day. A wife can show that she is available to be a part of her husband's life. If a wife seems uninterested, either through verbal or nonverbal communication, the husband will not be motivated to tell his wife about his life outside the home.

A wife can also involve her husband in her life and ask his advice. This does not mean that she has to bore him with many details that he cannot relate to, but rather, endeavor to make him understand how she spends her days. I once heard a *Rav* proclaim, "Share your days and you will share your lives."

**Message 15: Are we sharing our days?**

◆ Clarifying priorities

There will be many demands on your time. The main responsibility of maintaining the household rests on the woman. This includes cooking and cleaning, shopping, mending and organizing. In addition to taking care of your husband and children, you may have a job either inside or outside the home. Many *chesed* organizations will also request some of your time.

God willing, you will have children, and they occupy much time. It goes without saying that a wife must constantly remember to treat her husband as a priority. Organizational and volunteer work should only be taken on after home obligations are properly attended to. A husband enjoys coming home to a house that is a true home, not a place in disarray with a note that informs him that his wife is at a meeting.

Although the tasks of home maintenance may be tedious at times, they can take on a new significance when viewed as contributing to a sacred task — building and strengthening a *bayis ne'eman b'Yisrael.*

> Dina, a friend of mine, was asked to make knishes for a ladies' luncheon. Her immediate reaction was to say yes, but then she asked herself if her family could spare her for

the time it would take, and she decided that her husband and children rated above knishes on the priority list.

This is not to imply that community involvement is unimportant, just that one should keep things in perspective. It is acceptable to say that, although you feel that the cause is important, you are overextended at this time.

> Message 16: Are my husband and my home high on my priority list?

♦ Accepting your choices

After priorities have been set and reaffirmed, when a situation presents itself, there are choices to be made. Hopefully, you will make a choice based on the proper priorities.

> Ayala wants to go to a class. Her husband, Eli, has asked her to run an important errand that can only be done at the same time as the class. At first Ayala feels that she must go to the class. Then she realizes that she doesn't have to go. She can borrow another person's notes or tape of the class. She deliberates and comes to the conclusion that in this case the right choice is to forgo the class. If this is a choice that she cannot live with, then she should tell Eli how she feels, and hopefully a compromise can be reached.

If Ayala chooses the errand over the class, it is important that she not harbor resentment in her heart because her husband *made* her miss the class. She made her own decision to choose *shalom bayis*.

Often people think that they do not have the option of changing plans, when they actually do have other choices. In most instances there would not be any disastrous consequences if plans were modified. It is helpful for the wife to tell herself the following message, filling in the blank with the appropriate ending.

### Message 17: My marriage is more important than ... (my class, my telephone conversation, etc.).

Leah had her heart set on a new coat. Her husband, Chaim, didn't think that it was a purchase that they could afford, and he dismissed the idea. Leah communicated her feelings to him, and they discussed the matter, but Chaim maintained his objection. Hopefully she will be mature enough not to withhold her affections because of this. The constructive thing for her to tell herself is, "My marriage is more important than a coat." In addition to promoting *shalom bayis* and avoiding an argument, Leah is more likely to get what she wants in the future if she maintains an agreeable demeanor.

◆ Quality time

You have established your priorities and you are committed to uphold them. You make time for your husband and keep *shalom bayis* uppermost in your mind. It is important that you spend quality time with your husband and give him your full attention. (As we have said, husbands have similar obligations.) Often the amount of time spent is less important than the quality of time. Your husband deserves your full attention, and does not have to feel that your thoughts are elsewhere, or that you are waiting impatiently to get back to your other projects.

Many couples benefit greatly from occasionally going out together on a date, regardless of how long they have been married. Leaving the surroundings of the home provides a pleasant change of pace for the relationship. This is just one of the many ways that a couple can spend quality time together.

A student complained to a prominent *rosh yeshivah* that his wife expected him to call her every day from the yeshivah. The *rosh yeshivah* replied, "What's the problem? I call *my* wife every day."

Shelley, married for just a few months, complained to Mrs. Katz, "My husband, Yoni, works all day long and doesn't pay any attention to me. I asked him to write me little notes and leave them around the house and he said, 'Don't nag me.' Can't you please talk to him?"

Mrs. Katz is a wise woman, and she knows that it would be wrong to go over to Yoni and begin to lecture him. "Do you know what Shelley said about you? She says you don't pay any attention to her, and you only care about your work." If Mrs. Katz speaks to Yoni this way, she will put him on the defensive. He will be very upset to find out that Shelley has been talking about him to others. "Well," he might reply, "Shelley is so ungrateful. She doesn't appreciate anything I do. All she does is complain and nag. And do you think that she is so good to me? Well let me tell you what she does ..."

If Mrs. Katz thought that the situation was very serious, she might encourage Shelley to find a *Rav* or another qualified person to advise her. Shelley and Yoni could present their feelings, and the *Rav* or professional could then help each of them see what minor adjustments needed to be made in their relationship.

After some thought, Mrs. Katz decided that this situation could be improved in a more informal manner. She reminded Shelley that, rather than dwelling on what Yoni was not doing, she should focus on doing her part to promote *shalom bayis*.

Shelley took this advice and began to include notes in Yoni's lunch, as well as making other small gestures of affection and giving. She continued this for some time without becoming frustrated when she did not receive the same treatment in return. Eventually Yoni became more attentive and Shelley was very pleased with the results of her positive approach.

*Note:* Shelley shared private information about her marriage with Mrs. Katz. Was that appropriate? Assuming that Shelley felt that she needed some advice, then Shelley was correct to find one person to talk to. Shelley decided to speak to Mrs. Katz because she had always found Mrs. Katz to be a discreet woman who could analyze a given situation and suggest practical solutions. It is very good to work on a problem before it gets out of hand, and before a negative pattern is established. Hopefully Shelley did not discuss the situation with any of her friends, because that would not be productive.

### Message 18: Are we allowing time for our relationship?

A *kallah* who reads the stories of Leah and Shelley will tell herself, "That's not going to be me. My *chasan* and I get along very well, and we intend to keep it that way." Positive thinking is commendable, and it is even more effective if it is accompanied by an awareness of the components of a successful marriage. Armed with this knowledge, you can make a commitment at the beginning of your marriage to constantly maintain a high level in your relationship.

## Chapter Five
## Imperfect People

If all people were perfect, then the perfect marriage described in chapter 2 would be a common occurrence. As we all know, no one is perfect, and adjustments have to be made to accommodate human frailties and failings. No husband is perfect, neither is any wife. The goal in marriage is for the husband and wife to complement each other and help each other grow. Allowances should be made for the other's imperfections.

### ◆ You

You realize that you are not perfect. You know your shortcomings and are working to correct them. You should make allowances and excuse yourself when you slip and err. Take care not to fall into the trap of becoming depressed when you react the wrong way or make a mistake. It is much more productive to apologize politely, acknowledge to yourself that you are not perfect, and think of ways to correct the problem in the future.

You hope that your husband makes these allowances too. He realizes that you are trying your best to act properly and accepts you as you are. If he has not reached that level yet, accept his momentary disappointment and hope that the matter will blow over quickly. We need to pray to be smart enough to know what to pray for. One thing that is good for a wife to pray for is that her husband accept her as she is, despite her imperfections. Another prayer asks that she will have the patience to accept her husband with his imperfections.

**Message 19:** I am not perfect. Rather than pretend to be, I will apologize if the situation warrants it.

### ◆ Your husband

If there are no perfect people in the world, it stands to reason that your husband is not perfect either. *Hashem, in His infinite wisdom, gave you a husband with strengths that you need and imperfections that you can live with.* You may see these traits when you are engaged, but they do not deter you. One should strive to maintain the same acceptance after marriage. It is important to realize that, although now you know your *chasan* well enough to choose him, you will only really get to know him after you are married.

> Adina was newly married. She began to be bothered by a certain one of her husband's traits. Tuvia was constantly late for appointments. Adina was proud of the fact that she was always punctual, and this one flaw of her husband's truly upset her. If she starts calling him Mr. Late — even if only in her thoughts — then it means she is focusing on his imperfection. She would be much happier if she could tell herself, "I am not perfect. I will allow my husband to be imperfect, too. I find this trait to be very annoying, but if this is what Hashem has sent me, this is something I can live with. I am being given the opportunity to learn greater patience." Adina can also let Tuvia know in a pleasant manner that she really appreciates it when he is on time, and he may change his ways in response to the positive feedback.

If you repeat the following message to yourself when your husband does something wrong, you will do much to maintain *shalom bayis*.

Message 20: I do not demand perfection of my husband. If he slips, I forgive him.

◆ Respect

One of the most vital components of a healthy marriage is mutual respect. All people deserve respect because they are creations of the Creator. In addition, every person has some qualities that are very respectable. (They also have some undesirable qualities.) The goal is to develop tremendous respect for your husband, and not to let the little imperfections cause your respect to be diminished.

> Chana's husband was looking for a new position and he obtained a letter of reference from a teacher of his. Chana read the letter and was very impressed with the God-fearing, dedicated, caring, sincere man described in the letter. But she didn't think of her husband in those terms. In her mind he was sloppy and lazy. Which one was he? Both, of course, but Chana will have a much more successful marriage if she can respect her husband for his positive qualities and allow him to be imperfect.

There are certain qualities that one can respect easily. It is possible to train oneself, however, to respect other qualities too. If you are quick by nature, then speed might be a quality that you admire. Your husband might be slow and deliberate. Rather than lose respect for him, you can train yourself to admire slowness, since it often accompanies caution and thoroughness. Often the same quality that attracted you to your partner may be a quality that irks you later.

> Hadassah is worried and tense by nature. She became engaged to Nachum, who is quite easygoing. He helps

calm her down with his constant reassurances that situations will resolve themselves. When the invitations were late, Hadassah was frantic. Nachum confidently assured her, "Don't worry. It will all turn out fine."

After they are married for some time, Hadassah finds it difficult to respect Nachum because he is so unconcerned about everything. The baby is sick and all he says is, "It will probably be okay." The rent is late and he says, "Don't worry." Where is his sense of responsibility?

Hadassah would do well to start giving herself some messages. "My husband is a fine man, worthy of respect. He has a quality that I admire upon occasion. I respect him for his ability to calm me, as well as all his other positive qualities. However, I wish he showed greater concern in some instances. But I will allow him to be imperfect." She can also communicate the importance of concern in some areas, provided that she can speak pleasantly and respectfully.

Message 21: Every person has qualities worthy of respect. My husband has fine qualities. He is worthy of respect.

#### ◆ More about respect

There are two levels of respect. On the first level, every person should *treat* every other person with respect. Respect is evident in one's manner of speech and attitude.

Esti wanted her husband to move some chairs out of the way. "Move the chairs, Yossi," she barked. Her voice thinly veiled her disdain that he hadn't thought to move the chairs on his own, combined with a supercilious attitude that *she* was wise enough to think of it. How different things would have been if she'd said, "Yossi dear, please do me a favor and move the chairs. Thank you. I really appreciate your help."

The second level of respect is to *feel* respect toward others. If one does not feel respect for a husband, it is difficult to treat him with respect. A wife should still treat her husband with respect, even if she doesn't truly feel that respect. At the same time she should endeavor to acquire that feeling. How does one come to feel respect? How can feelings be regulated? If a wife focuses on the positive aspects of her husband, she will become more respectful of him.

*The concept of relating to a husband with respect cannot be overemphasized.* A husband who is treated with respect is the king of his castle. He has a fortress that he can escape to at the end of a day. A husband who is greeted with disdain and contempt will find it difficult to face the world and he'll look to escape from his prison-like home. He may then lash out at his wife and a negative cycle will start.

Message 22: Do I treat my husband with respect? Do I feel respect toward him?

### ♦ Change

It is well known that when a couple marries, both the husband and the wife are supposed to accept their respective spouses as they are. It is unwise to marry someone on the assumption that you can change him. Of course you may wish him to change in certain areas and think of clever ways to facilitate that change. But remember, change takes time, motivation, and support. If you allow for all of those, you will hopefully see results.

Prayer is a significant factor here, too. If you pray on behalf of your husband, requesting that he be assisted in his character growth, you are approaching the One Who can help.

Prayer has an additional advantage. If you pray for someone, then you feel more positively about him. He becomes someone that you are trying to help, not someone you want to find fault with.

Avraham had a tendency to anger easily. His wife, Bat-sheva, accepted him as he was. She respected him for his other fine qualities and realized that she had to allow for his flaw. After several years of marriage, she was pleased to see that he had calmed down considerably. She attributed it to several factors. Firstly, Avraham had made a conscious effort to grow and change in this area. Secondly, Batsheva had never verbally attacked him when he became angry, and had supported his efforts at improvement. She didn't magnify his momentary failures, and her calm nature served as an example to him.

Upon occasion, change will come after marriage. Either the husband or the wife will display a new trait or preference, one that is not welcome. This, too, has to be accepted and then dealt with in the most productive way.

Shimon always enjoyed having guests over on Shabbos and the guests had been a major part of Shabbos. Recently, Shimon has changed and he no longer is interested in having guests. "Wait a minute," thinks his wife, Tzipporah. "This is not what I expected when I married him. The Shimon I married enjoyed guests." Tzipporah can best deal with this situation by accepting and respecting him despite this one area. Then she can address the issue of guests. Perhaps a compromise can be reached and guests will be invited only on an occasional basis. Perhaps Shimon is ready for a different type of guest. Perhaps he needs a month or two without guests. Perhaps Shimon assessed the situation and decided that the family needs more private time on Shabbos.

Message 23: People change and have different needs at different times in their lives.

♦ A recommendation

There is a simple technique that can help make it easier to respect and appreciate your husband. Upon waking in the morning, you should say, "Thank you Hashem for sending me such a wonderful husband." If a wife feels gratitude to Hashem for sending her the husband that she has, then she focuses on his good qualities. Conversely, if she considers her husband less than adequate, she is ungrateful to Hashem.

Hashem has presented you with the most befitting person, the completion of your *neshamah.* Surely you can find something in him to thank Hashem for. To clarify, every husband or wife has faults, but each one is basically good and is a precious gift from Hashem.

> I went to visit Debbie, who was sitting *shivah* for her husband. Her husband had been sick for many years and passed away in the prime of his life. "I had a gem," she said, "and I lost him. But at least I had him for as long as I did." My heart went out to this grieving wife, who sharply felt the loss of her precious husband. She truly had a gem, and she appreciated him during his lifetime. But how many people only discover their gems when it is too late?

**Message 24: Did I thank Hashem for my husband today?**

◆ Self-esteem

People mistakenly equate self-esteem with haughtiness and self-pride. This is far from the truth. People who have a good sense of themselves are comfortable with who they are and their God-given talents. They do not rely on others for approval, and do not need to prove their worth to the world. A person who has self-esteem will not be insulted by derogatory comments, nor will he be afraid to compromise and yield his point. He realizes that his sense of self-worth is not diminished if he compromises.

Many people have poor self-esteem, and do not perceive themselves as being talented and worthwhile. Unfortunately, a person who views himself as a loser will turn out to be a loser.

Someone who needs clarification as to his or her self-worth can investigate the Torah perspective of the topic by discussing the matter with a knowledgeable person or reading one of the books available on the topic.*

A marriage is enhanced and not, *chas v'shalom*, damaged if both spouses possess self-esteem. A wife can do much to build up her husband's sense of self-worth if she believes in him. Conversely, her lack of respect can cause him to feel worthless, and it may manifest itself in his making demands in a desperate attempt to prove himself.

> Shmeil says, "From now on I want to see some more respect around here. After all, I am the man of the house. I have decided that we are going to visit my parents today, and I don't want any argument."
>
> What Shmeil really is saying (although he probably doesn't realize it himself) is that he doesn't feel that his opinion is valued, so he is going to forcibly attempt to get his way.

**Message 25: An accurate sense of self-worth is an asset to a marriage.**

◆ Serious problems

One note of caution. In some instances there are serious personality problems that should be attended to. These problems may be the result of childhood trauma, family relationships, or many other possible factors. Although a supportive, respectful wife is helpful to someone with these problems, outside help is sometimes required. A *Rav* should be consulted. This *Rav* may feel that professional counseling would be advantageous.

> Dr. Gross, a successful doctor, had just lost his father. He was understandably upset and depressed. Some time had passed and Dr. Gross felt that he was grieving excessively.

---

\* *Let Us Make Man*, by Rabbi Dr. Abraham J. Twerski, is one such book.

He discussed the matter with his *Rav*, and was advised to seek professional help. After a few sessions, the problem was resolved.

If a wife feels that her husband's reactions and difficulties are such that outside help is needed, she should think carefully about how to present the topic. It must be done delicately, and the message must be communicated that her sole interest is to see her husband get the help he needs, and not to label him as "troubled." Mrs. Gross was fortunate that her husband realized his problem on his own, and she did not have to be the one to suggest that he get help.

Message 26: There are some problems that require outside help.

Although the results won't show immediately, mutual effort toward accepting and respecting each other will help a couple to grow together and appreciate each other for what they are.

*Chapter Six*
# How to Talk to Your Husband

How does one talk to a husband? The answer to this question is really quite simple and any *kallah* can supply the proper response. A spouse is to be treated with respect. Both husband and wife deserve the same courtesy as any other human being. The tone of voice one uses when imparting a message is as important as the message itself. A polite, dignified manner is an asset to *shalom bayis*. In fact, a *kallah* might wonder why there is any need for a chapter to elaborate on this topic. However, sometimes it is good to restate the obvious.

◆ A pleasant manner

A husband should be spoken to in a pleasant manner, simply because it is the right thing to do. Everyone should be spoken to in a calm, pleasant manner. As an added plus, one's message will be more readily received if it is presented properly. If a husband gets the message, "I love you and respect you and I would like to inform you of something for our mutual benefit," he is likely to listen. If he gets the message that he doesn't merit the common decency that you show others, chances are that the request that you make will be for nothing.

One technique to help people speak in a pleasant tone of voice is for them to imagine that their voices are being recorded and will be played back. If they listen carefully to how they sound, they can assess if they sound the way they intended.

> Rivka picks up the phone and dials her friend, Ora. Ora is a cheerful woman who always is friendly and polite. Little Shmuel, Ora's son, answers the phone. Rivka is surprised to hear Ora yelling in the background. Ora finally comes to the phone and excuses herself. "Hello, Rivka," she says in a sweet, calm voice. "I was just explaining something to my husband." Rivka may wonder what she has done to deserve such a friendly greeting, or rather what Ora's husband has done to be spoken to in such an inappropriate manner.

**Message 27: The tone of a conversation is as important as the message.**

### ◆ Maintain your island

When an issue needs discussing, a wise wife knows that even a politely stated complaint should be voiced only in private. No one else should have to hear your personal disagreements. Nor should you bring these complaints to other members of the family or friends. In some specific instances it is beneficial to find one wise person that you trust who can objectively listen to a problem and suggest some insights. It is advantageous to discuss a problematic situation with this one person, but not with many curious friends. This confidante has to be careful not to believe your story, but to listen carefully to your perception of the situation so that he or she can advise you effectively.

This option should be used with much forethought, taking care to find a truly objective person who will be able to give constructive advice. Requesting advice from a wise mentor has nothing in common with venting frustrations to a friend. In the first case one is looking for guidance. In the second case it is sympathy that is sought.

Message 28: Do I remember that discussions are to be kept private?

◆ Discuss issues, not people

There are certain factors to keep in mind in any productive discussion:

*1. Avoid blame.*

The issue is not who is responsible for the problem, but how is the couple going to prevent it from recurring.

> The front door was not locked one night. Listed below are two discussions. The first one will exacerbate the situation whereas the second one can prevent the problem in the future.
>
> Approach #1 (blame). She: "Why didn't you remember to lock the door?" He: "Why are you blaming me? I always lock the door; just this once I forgot. You never are concerned with safety in this house."
>
> Approach #2 (without blame). She: "It seems that we forgot to lock the door last night. Let us think of a way to remind ourselves so that it doesn't happen again." He: "Perhaps we can leave a little note where we will see it before we go to bed."
>
> Shmuel was watching the children. All of a sudden three-year-old Aryeh leaned on the stroller. The baby fell onto the concrete sidewalk and needed stitches. Avigayil's initial reaction was to blame Shmuel, but she knew that would be unproductive and that accidents do happen. All the way to the hospital she told herself, "I will not blame Shmuel. I don't watch the children every second, and the same thing could have happened when I was outside with them." By the time she came home, she could greet Shmuel civilly. He began apologizing for his neglect and

Avigayil was very proud of herself that she was able to say, "Don't worry. These things can happen to anyone." Imagine how different things would have been if Avigayil had come home and blamed Shmuel.

*2. Avoid "never" and "always" and "...est" statements.*
These statements are usually exaggerations and confrontational.

"You never care about my feelings!" Is that really true? Never?

"You always ignore me." Always?

"You are the laziest..." Is he really the most lazy?

*3. Comparisons are to be avoided.*
"Everyone else remembers birthdays."

"My father would never have reacted that way."

*4. Don't attack.*
"Why are you so immature that you keep bickering with my parents." Instead of attacking your spouse, deal with the issue. "How can we resolve the problem between you and my parents?"

*5. Share responsibility.*
The above example also demonstrates another point. A wife should try to guide such conversations into a deliberation of what a couple can do together to solve a problem, rather than letting it become one spouse attacking the other.

*6. "I" messages are to be used whenever possible.*
An "I" message focuses on what you want or need, rather than on what he didn't do. "I appreciate it when I get my telephone messages." Compare that to: "Why don't you ever give me my telephone messages?"

---

**Message 29:** I will try to avoid hurtful comments and focus on the issues at hand.

### ◆ A regal family

You may wonder: What if he doesn't talk to me properly? Do I still have to treat him so well? The answer is yes, yes, yes. It does not say in the Torah, "Love your friend if he treats you properly." It says, "Love your friend" — unconditionally, no matter how he treats you. Of course, it is easier to treat others well when they treat you well, and much more of a test when they forget their manners. If you treat your husband like a king, he will come to treat you like a queen. Your royal family will develop over time. Communication is important here also.

> Rena does not appreciate her husband Zev's complaints. "Why don't you have supper ready when I come home? Why didn't you buy that item that I needed, etc., etc."
>
> Rena remembers to respond to Zev's comments pleasantly, although it is very hard to do. She realizes that his inappropriate behavior does not exempt her from treating him properly. She also knows that there is a greater likelihood that she will rectify the situation if she does not create a cycle of verbal abuse.
>
> At one point, Rena calmly but firmly says, "I find it very difficult to deal with comments that are spoken in an angry manner. I would appreciate it if you could let me know what is bothering you in a more pleasant fashion."

Zev really loves his wife and this statement will hopefully make him realize that his actions were hurtful. If Rena had attacked Zev ("Why are you so nasty?") or branded him as hopeless through her generalizations ("You never talk nicely to me!"), then her message would have been missed. Zev would have reacted defensively. He would say to himself, "Who does she think she is? Is she perfect? She deserves the way I talk to her! If she wouldn't be so irresponsible, I wouldn't have to talk that way."

## Message 30: Am I nurturing a regal family?

It is evident from the above discussion that we must think before we speak. This is a skill that can be learned. It is also helpful to try to look at things the way your husband would, and imagine just how your words would be received by him. Words that were not meant to hurt may be hurtful to some people. If you tell your husband that he is unfeeling, you may mean that he does not express his emotions as much as you would like, but he may interpret it to mean that you think he is cruel. It is not easy to take all these things into consideration before speaking, but it is definitely worth the effort.

*Chapter Seven*

*Proper Perspectives*

When someone is in the midst of a situation, it is easy for him to blow things out of proportion. If people learn to put things into perspective, then they do not dwell on minor incidents. When life is viewed as a long road headed in the right direction, it is easier to ignore brief deviations from this road.

◆ A message to kallahs

I once gave a class on the topic of *shalom bayis*. I asked the women there individually to think of ten positive qualities their husbands possessed. I expected them to ponder or to quickly begin compiling a list. Imagine my surprise when they all began to laugh. Laughter is an inappropriate reaction to the request.

Why did they laugh? They all had been married for a while, and they had unfortunately fallen into the bad habit of focusing on their husband's negative qualities. (This is the man who forgot to take out the garbage. This is the man who raises his voice to the children.) They had not given much thought recently to all the positive aspects of their wonderful husbands.

As a *kallah*, this is hard to imagine. When you are asked to describe your *chasan*, many positive descriptions come to mind. When these women married, they also had good things to readily say about their *chasanim*. Did these men change? Probably not. When you live with someone, you see all of his qualities. That doesn't mean that positive qualities disappear, but negative qualities surface as well. People must remember to make a conscious effort to focus on the positive.

> Message 31: I will try to focus on my husband's positive qualities (and I hope that he will try to focus on mine).

### ◆ The little things

What are the main causes of frustration in a marriage? Usually the couple does not have major disagreements and problems. Small nuisances and little details cause people to be upset at one another. She forgot to buy a new light bulb. He came late to pick her up. The list of small mistakes a person can make is endless. If you are upset with your spouse, it is helpful to pinpoint the exact cause of your upset, and then to analyze whether it is important enough to mar *shalom bayis.*

> At a fiftieth wedding anniversary celebration, the wife was asked what she thought was the secret to her marital success. She replied, "When I got married, I told myself that I would ignore the first ten things that my husband did wrong. Whenever I reached the ninth one, I discarded the list and started again, allowing him another ten things. We have been living peacefully this way for fifty years."
>
> "Let me give a concrete example," continued the woman. "Early in our marriage there was the time that my husband emptied the garbage can but did not return it to the proper corner. I will admit I initially felt upset, but then I reminded myself that this was one of the "first ten things." I would overlook this event. In order to help

myself ignore the situation, I focused on the positive. At least he took out the garbage. I also can tell you that, in fifty years of marriage, where the garbage can is placed occupies virtually no importance."

Everyone chuckled as the story was recounted. Surely they would not get upset over such a minor event. Hopefully they would remember their resolve when they arrived home, and adopt this attitude on a long-term basis.

Here is a message that you can repeat to yourself to help put things in perspective:

Message 32: Is this important enough that it will bother me twenty years from now, five years from now, or even next week?

♦ Objectivity

Often we react inappropriately when we are personally affected by something. If the same thing occurred to a friend, we'd probably consider it insignificant. If we could learn to view a situation objectively, as if we were watching a show, we would see things in perspective.

Bluma and Elchanan were preparing to leave for a wedding. Elchanan kept hurrying Bluma, "We'll be late and miss the *chuppah*!" Bluma was doing her best to get ready on time, and left feeling rather rushed. They arrived at the wedding more than a half-hour after the time that the *chuppah* was scheduled for, but in fact, the *chuppah* had not yet begun. Bluma glanced down at her feet and noticed that she had forgotten to change her shoes. She became very angry at Elchanan. "It's his fault that I have to feel so embarrassed. Everyone will notice that my shoes don't match my dress!" she thought. "Why does he always rush me? I knew we wouldn't miss the *chuppah*."

If Bluma could look at the situation objectively, as if it had happened to someone else, she would come to a different conclusion. Elchanan was not unreasonable in wanting to get to the *chuppah* on time. It is also not his fault that Bluma forgot to change her shoes. Why should Bluma get upset at her husband because she is late and forgetful?

Elchanan and/or Bluma could spend a few minutes thinking about how to avoid a similar occurrence in the future. Assuming that Elchanan would like to be at the *chasunah* at seven o'clock, he can tell Bluma that he will be ready to leave at six. This way he compensates for her tendency to be late. If Bluma's schedule does not allow her to be ready when her husband wants to leave, perhaps they can arrive at the *chasunah* independently. Again, a problem-solving, practical approach accomplishes much more than blame and anger.

Below is a message to repeat whenever your husband does something that you consider to be "wrong," and you feel annoyed by it.

> **Message 33:** If I heard that my friend's husband did this thing, would I think that she was right to be so upset with him, or would I think that my friend was overreacting?

### ◆ Attributing motives

Most people's misdeeds are not done deliberately to hurt other people. Usually the action was done thoughtlessly or carelessly. While it is true that, ideally, people should always be sensitive and thoughtful, care must be taken not to attach too much significance to small mistakes.

> Yossi wore a tie that he knew his wife disliked. He did not do it because he doesn't think that her opinions are important. He wore it because it was the first tie that he found, and he was in a rush.

> Sara cooked fish for supper, not because she wanted to make her husband angry; she forgot that he disliked fish.

Chana loves flowers and has hinted many times that she would love to get flowers for Shabbos. Daniel has never taken the hint. The fact that he doesn't buy flowers does not prove that he doesn't love Chana. It proves that he doesn't love flowers.

Message 34: Am I attributing to others motives that do not exist?

◆ Allowances for a bad day

Anyone can have a bad day. If you notice that your husband is upset about something, or he seems moody, expect him to overreact and slip from his normally fine character.

If you are not feeling well one day, wouldn't you like to say, "Please ignore what I say. I feel jumpy today. Blame it on my sinuses." Allow him the same privilege. It is advisable to stay clear of controversial topics on those days.

> "Shlomo, I wanted to talk about our budget, specifically whether we can increase the clothing budget."
>
> "Gitty, I had a rough day at work. Let's discuss it at a different time."
>
> "Shlomo, we've pushed this discussion off before and I really want to buy a few things before *Yom Tov*."

It is easy to see that Gitty would be much wiser to postpone her discussion just a bit longer.

Message 35: I will make allowances if my husband has a bad day.

◆ The total picture

A husband should be viewed as a total person. Rather than focus on the small things that he does wrong, see the overall picture. "He never listens to me": Probably he doesn't listen sometimes, but often he does. "He is not as sensitive as I would like": Yes, but he is very involved in all sorts of *chesed* projects, and people always ask his advice.

> It was four o'clock. Freidy was entertaining company who had just arrived from out-of-town. She placed some cookies, drinks and nosh on the table. As she and her husband Shaya sat chatting with the guests, their two-year-old son Dovie wandered in and gravitated toward the cookies. He reached his little hand up and helped himself to one. When his hand reached up for a second cookie, Freidy said, "Okay, but this is the last cookie before supper. I don't want you to ruin your appetite."
>
> This logic was beyond the comprehension of a two year old, and soon he was back for a third cookie. "No," said Freidy. "Remember what we said. No more cookies until after supper."
>
> Shaya observed his sad little son staring at the cookie plate. "Here, Dovie," he said, "have another cookie."
>
> Anyone who ever read a book on child care would have been horrified. Shaya had just violated a major rule in child rearing. He had disregarded a rule that his wife made, and contradicted her in front of her son and in front of company.
>
> How did Freidy react? She looked at her husband with a mixture of love and exasperation. "That's my imperfect husband," she seemed to be thinking. "He is wonderful and kind and wise, but he didn't learn this rule yet."
>
> She was careful not to attribute motives. She realized that Shaya did not contradict her because he lacked respect for her. He just was motivated by his sympathy for his little two year old, who wanted the cookies that were on the table.

If she wants to prevent this incident from recurring, Freidy might calmly say to her husband at some time in the future, "Please do not break my rules with the children. It confuses them." If the discussion ends there, *shalom bayis* will be the true winner. It is easy to see how one cookie could cause a major fight if each side only focused on the principle and refused to bend.

> Message 36: Do I put my husband's failings in perspective, and realize that he is basically good?

◆ Allowing for idiosyncrasies

Everyone has his own idiosyncrasies. These behaviors or requests may not be logical, but the need for them is ingrained in a person. If a husband's idiosyncrasies affect only him and not others, do not let them diminish your respect for him. If he makes demands on you that you consider to be illogical, it is often easier to go along with them than to challenge each one. For example, if a husband requests that a certain kind of napkin be used, using that kind is a small step toward *shalom bayis.*

Occasionally, these requests about details are not illogical, but just not important to you. One husband may establish a rule that the car should be filled with gas whenever the gauge shows that the tank is one-quarter full. If the wife is careful to take notice and comply, in addition to avoiding conflict, she also will not run out of gas.

◆ Analyzing requirements

You, too, may have requirements which your husband thinks are *meshugasin.* Many things do not fall within the category of absolutely right or wrong; they are simply preferences that you grew up with. If you strongly believe that gas should be put in the car when the tank is one-quarter full, and your husband won't comply, give some thought to whether this is something that you will continue to demand. The same example was used here in both cases to point out that you should respect your husband's wishes if you cannot convince him to forgo them, but you should be selective about which of your own wishes you require of him.

Why is it recommended that you drop as many demands as you can? Is this to negate the importance of your feelings? The goal is *shalom bayis* and both husband and wife have to train themselves to swallow their personal pride in favor of making the marriage work. Hopefully your husband has been trained as well as you, and he refrains from making excessive demands. In addition, one who is willing to drop his smaller demands will more likely have his valid ones met. If your husband feels that he has given in to your last hundred demands, he may balk at number 101, which could be something that you really wanted.

**Message 37: Am I making too many unnecessary demands?**

Many problems can be solved if they are viewed as challenges. People enjoy a challenge. The situation can be analyzed and creative solutions found if objectivity is maintained.

> Chedva had a problem. Levi kept inviting Shabbos guests without consulting her. No, she didn't think that she had a problem — she had a challenge. Chedva was careful not to get angry at Levi (chapter 10) and she allowed him to be imperfect (chapter 5). However, she did not appreciate guests being invited without her knowledge. She analyzed the situation objectively, as if she were giving advice to someone else. Was she more bothered by the fact that she wasn't being consulted, or the fact that she didn't know how much food to cook? She decided to accept the fact that her husband was permitted to do some things without consulting her, and focused on how to get Levi to report to her how many guests were coming.
>
> Chedva began to think of creative solutions. She remembered to ask Levi on Wednesday for a guest count, and didn't rely on him to remember to report everyone

he had invited. After a while Chedva encouraged Levi to give guests a tentative invitation and say that he had to check with his wife before making it final. Chedva learned that the problem was solvable once she thought of it as a challenge that she could surmount.

It is often difficult to maintain the proper perspective. The above suggestions of maintaining objectivity and making allowances are very helpful. A sense of humor is also an asset to a couple. Rather than dwell on every incident, sometimes a laugh and a joke can help the couple realize the relative insignificance of a matter.

Upon occasion, however, a husband and wife do not see eye to eye on a major matter and, instead of working together toward a common goal, they begin to turn against each other. It may be a simple issue that could be resolved with some solid advice. People are not embarrassed to ask halachic questions of a *Rav*. When dealing in areas of interpersonal relationships, people should also ask him for advice and guidance. Often a couple will come to a *Rav* only after their relationship has deteriorated to a dangerous point. They would have been much better off if they had set matters straight at the beginning of the disagreement.

If someone is traveling to an unfamiliar destination, and has made a wrong turn, it is much better to ask directions as soon as the mistake is noticed than to find out four hours later. The longer a disagreement goes on, the more chance of hurtful comments and damage to the marriage. A *Rav, Rebbe*, or former teacher usually is quite willing to help. Often, just discussing the issues in the presence of another person gives both partners the opportunity to express their feelings in a constructive manner.

*Chapter Eight*

*Coping*

The ability to cope with life is a skill that is beneficial to everyone, not only to *kallah*s. Life is replete with stressful situations, and peace of mind is dependent on one's ability to cope and deal with these situations. People who have difficulty coping with daily life often place a strain on their relationships with others. Therefore, this chapter has been included in a book addressed to *kallah*s. One who learns how to accept situations in a calm and positive manner will have peace of mind, and will be able to relate to others, including a spouse, in a peaceful manner. In addition, many health problems are caused or aggravated by one's inability to deal properly with stress. The ability to cope with stress is therefore an asset to one's emotional and physical health, as well as to one's relationships.

◆ Stress

There are many causes of stress in life. A situation that is very stressful for one person may not be as stressful for another, but there are certain basic types of stress-producing events that affect us all. Change is stressful. People become accustomed to one pattern, and when a situation changes, stress can occur. This does not mean that every change is disastrous or dangerous, but people should allow for greater stress when they experience a major change in routine, such as a move to a new city. Deadlines, money worries, tiredness, and illnesses are all stress producing, as are major events in life. A wedding, the birth of a child, a holiday, or a new job are all wonderful events, but they can cause stress.

> I'm sure that you have met Mrs. F.E. Pesach. [That stands for Frantic *Erev Pesach.*] She is tense and nervous; her blood pressure is up and her indigestion has become worse. She is experiencing difficulty sleeping at night — all due to her pre-Pesach frenzy. In her stressful state, she barks orders to her children and rants at her husband.
>
> It is easy to see why preparing for Pesach is so stressful. It contains many stress producers. There are deadlines to be met, overtiredness to deal with, and a sincere desire to create a halachically *chametz*-free house. But does it really have to be this way? In her desire to comply with the Torah prohibition against *chametz*, is Mrs. F.E. Pesach permitted to forget about pleasant speech and *shalom bayis*?

**Message 38: I will try to anticipate stress-producing situations and be prepared for them.**

◆ Coping with stress

Identifying stress is just the beginning. After a situation has been identified as stressful, there are three main ways in which to deal with it. You may try to (1) calm yourself, (2) change the circumstances, and/or (3) change your reaction to it.

*Calming yourself (step 1)*

There are several ways to calm down when under stress. Some people benefit most from a nap, others are calmed by a walk in the fresh air, exercise, music or a diverting activity. These things do not solve any problems, but they can lower a person's stress level. As it has been pointed out here, when someone is under stress, he or she tends to be jumpy and may not speak to a spouse properly. If people can identify stress and do things to keep themselves calm, *shalom bayis* is enhanced.

### Changing the circumstances (step 2)

Often the stress-producing situation can be changed. Mrs. F.E. Pesach might try starting her preparations earlier. She might also be able to shorten her list to include those things that are necessary for making Pesach, and leave spring cleaning for another time.

### Changing your reactions (step 3)

Many times a situation cannot be changed. In those cases, there are methods of changing your reaction to it. When one is confronted with a stressful situation, a possible reaction is to despair of success. "I can't do this," says the overwhelmed person. One who is convinced that she *is* capable of accomplishing a difficult task is more likely to succeed. This confidence can stem from a reevaluation of a difficult event. Instead of being classified as unbearable, it can be redefined as difficult but livable.

For instance, an upcoming event that appears overwhelming can be broken into parts and hence made to feel manageable. The tasks can be listed and checked off as they are accomplished.

> Mina and her husband are organizing *sheva berachos* for friends. Mina is quite nervous and wonders if she will be able to produce a successful affair. She realizes that a calm demeanor will be advantageous, and decides to approach the situation in an organized manner. She makes a list of the items she needs to purchase, the menu, and the various tasks to be done. She includes the approximate time necessary to take care of each item. After thinking it

all through and listing the tasks on paper, she realizes that she is capable of managing the affair. She now approaches preparations for the *sheva berachos* with confidence and a positive attitude.

This confidence can also stem from a positive sense of self. "I can handle this situation." People usually rise to meet their own self-assessment of their capabilities. Conversely, they are limited by their own self-doubts.

One technique that can be employed, either alone or in conjunction with the above-mentioned recommendations, is to paint a mental picture of success. The person imagines in detail how she will approach the situation in a calm manner. The person who can envision success will come closer to achieving that success.

Chana finds bedtime stressful. By the time her children are finally in bed, she feels drained. She decides to give some thought to the situation and make the bedtime routine flow more smoothly. Chana imagines how she wishes to react to her children's antics and envisions herself calmly attending to each child, taking their behavior in stride.

The next evening, Chana is determined to act in the calm manner that she has pictured. Although the children behave as they have done in the past, her mental image helps her remain unflustered.

Another technique is to adopt a "what would be if" approach. In this approach, we consider the worst and realize that it can be dealt with. The key to all these above-mentioned methods is to be in control of our thoughts. When a stressful situation occurs, we can calm ourselves by repeating positive thoughts.

Miriam and Zvi are planning a move to a new city. There are a myriad of details to attend to, and Miriam is completely overwhelmed and "stressed out." She yells at the

children and blames her husband for circumstances beyond his control. Miriam finds herself bothered by tension
headaches.

Then Miriam decides to take mental control of her
stress reaction. First she acknowledges the stress and
decides that she must take some action to relieve it. (1)
She chooses to sit for five minutes, taking deep breaths
while listening to calming music. (2) She does not want
the situation to change in this case. She wants to move.
(3) So the situation will remain the same, but Miriam's
ability to cope with the move will be improved if she
can control her stress reaction. She begins talking to
herself. "This situation is not unbearable. We can succeed
in this move. Certainly there are many things I have to
do, but I can make a list and attack them one at a time.
Furthermore, it would not be so tragic if I didn't organize
the clothes before I packed them."

Miriam can then paint a mental picture of success.
She can envision herself waking up each day in a calm
frame of mind and pleasantly attending to all the necessary details of the move. This positive imagery can serve
as a model for Miriam as she attends to packing with new-
found calm.

Message 39: When I feel stress I will apply the three-step plan.
1. I will find a way of physically relieving the stress;
2. I will try to change the situation;
3. Then I will think positively and replace my stressful reaction
with calming thoughts.

### ◆ The workplace

The workplace is full of stress. There are deadlines to meet
and co-workers to deal with. Women who work outside
the home have to cope with the strains of a job in addition to maintaining their homes. When choosing a job or
profession, it is important to consider how stressful the
job will be and how much the pressures of the job will

intrude on one's home life. There is a survival skill that can help a woman cope with the demands of her many tasks — compartmentalization. Compartmentalization is the ability to place tasks and events into different mental compartments. When at work, she focuses on work. When she gets home, she focuses on her home and family, having mentally left her work at the job site.

Another skill that helps people cope with work is the ability to organize their time. When a woman works outside the home, she has a limited amount of time to attend to her home responsibilities. If she is organized, she can accomplish a greater amount in the time that is available.

The ability to develop a calm attitude toward events is also a great asset to anyone, especially the working woman. When someone is on a tight time schedule, unexpected crises and problems create a real challenge. If these annoying events are viewed calmly as inconveniences, the woman will be able to continue with her routine. If these unscheduled events truly unnerve her, then she will find juggling a work schedule and a home schedule very difficult.

Sara, a teacher, was prepared to leave for work one morning. The children were in the car, since Sara brought them to a babysitter daily. As Sara turned the key in the ignition, it became apparent that the car would not cooperate. Sara glanced at the clock and realized that she still had ten minutes in which to cope with this unexpected turn of events. She quickly brought the children inside so they wouldn't have to wait in the cold car, and began to make some phone calls. She soon found a lift for herself as well as a different ride for her children. She decided that she would attend to her car trouble after work, and arrived there with three minutes to spare. She managed to concentrate on her work and teach an inspiring lesson despite the morning's events.

A woman is also affected by the stress of her husband's job. He, too, ought to leave his work problems at the office, and pay full attention to his family once he comes home. However, it may be difficult for him to do that. A wife who is aware of the problem can help her husband find ways to relieve his job-related stress. Perhaps he just needs a few minutes to relax as soon as he comes home, before hearing about all the problems of the day.

> Mr. and Mrs. Levy have been married for many years. They have worked together in the same family business for the last fifteen years. They both agree on one important family rule. When the Levys arrive home after a day's work, they close the door on the business world and do not discuss any topics that are work-related. This gives them the opportunity to relax from the stresses of the business.

Message 40: I will be aware of job-related stress, try to compartmentalize, and encourage my husband to do the same.

### ◆ Children

Raising children is a large topic that is beyond the scope of this book. Included in this section are just a few thoughts on children that relate directly to *shalom bayis*. It is difficult for newly marrieds to envision that, God willing, one day in the not-too-distant future they will be parents. With the addition of a child, there is a major shift in focus. There is now a new person demanding much attention. It is important for a new mother to make sure that she doesn't inadvertently ignore her husband.

There are many additional chores to be done when there are little ones in the house. How much should the husband help with these chores? The answer to that question is very individual. There are some households where the husband does the shopping, others in which he has a major role in child care, or helps with the cooking, and still others where the husband is occupied with his own pursuits and does not help appreciably. If a situation arises where the wife feels overwhelmed and frustrated, then she should communicate her feelings — without blame and disdain — and hopefully a solution will be found. It is good to keep in mind that there are certain jobs that men find easier to do, and it is more productive to give someone a job that he will execute willingly.

> Nachum, a very busy man, is also a very helpful husband. He takes care of the three little children so his wife Eti can take a nap in the afternoon. He feeds the children and makes his own lunch.
>
> Simcha, also a busy man, does almost nothing in the house. I was at Simcha and Devorah's house and a cold drink had been served in the dining room. A few minutes later Devorah noticed the glasses had been brought to the sink. She asked me if I had done it and I informed her that her husband had brought them in. Her face showed great surprise. It was obvious that Simcha was not in the habit of clearing the table. Later in the conversation, the situation was clarified. "I don't expect Simcha to help around the house," she explained. "That is my job. He works full time and is president of the shul. Why would I burden him with more?"

Is Simcha bad and Nachum good? As long as Eti and Devorah are both satisfied, they are both good. But look at the case of Naomi and Ari.

> Both Naomi and Ari work full time. She arrives home at four o'clock and has to give the children some attention and rush to prepare supper. Ari arrives home at five o'clock and sits down in his easy chair with the newspaper in order to relax from his hard day at work. Naomi is frustrated and upset. How can he just sit there when she is exhausted and overworked? Ari is perplexed. All he wants is to sit for a few minutes and unwind from his hard day. Why does Naomi always bark orders at him as soon as

he comes home? Clearly, communication is lacking here, as well as a genuine attempt to understand each other's needs. Hopefully Ari can be made to understand that indeed Naomi is overworked and needs his help before supper. The message should also be conveyed to Ari that Naomi appreciates the help that he gives at other times. Naomi, on the other hand, should be made to understand that Ari views his home as his refuge from the world, and he needs a calm environment when he comes home.

Naomi and Ari ought to discuss the situation and reach a solution that is acceptable to both of them. Perhaps if Ari takes a few minutes to relax when he comes home, he will then be ready to help.

It is possible that when a couple discusses household chores, a wife will discover that her husband thinks that housework is a wife's job, and he does not intend to help as much as she would like. (A European woman in her sixties told me that when her children were small, it was unheard of for a husband to help with the household chores.) Rather than experience mounting resentment toward her husband, the wife should view the situation as a challenge. How can she find a clever way to make him change his attitude? Perhaps expressing appreciation to her husband for whatever help she receives will motivate him to help more. Taking counsel with a *Rav* or advisor can be productive. Until the wife is able to succeed in affecting a change in her husband's attitude, she is best off making peace with the situation as it is. She should tell herself that her husband has many fine points. He is not helpful, but she will accept him even though she thinks that he is making an unwise decision. If she assumes that the household jobs are her responsibility, and for some reason he is unable to join her, then she will not be upset at him for constantly not helping.

If a husband is not helpful enough, a wife can hope and pray that he will soon embark upon a course of self-improvement to refine his trait of helpfulness.

It is also possible that the husband is helpful, but the wife is making excessive demands on her husband's time, and not considering his other obligations. Objective analysis of the situation along with determination on the part of the couple to clarify matters together is very important here.

◆ Recommendations for mothers of small children

Many mothers of infants and small children stay at home with them all day. It is wonderful for the children to be raised by their own mother who loves them. It is also very rewarding for a mother to see her child grow and blossom.

However, it is a fact that many women find the adjustment to staying home difficult. They are surprised they feel frustrated staying home all day with these precious little ones. One of the causes of this frustration is the fact that a young wife is accustomed to activities that require mental effort, and many of the chores associated with child care are in essence routine jobs. One way to surmount this problem is to realize that each thing done for a baby is really a *chesed*. The baby is helpless to do these things for himself. He relies on his mother to provide life-sustaining food, and to attend to all his needs. Can any job entail more responsibility and prestige?

Another suggestion is to imagine which situation would make you happy, and to imagine in detail how you really wish things were. In most cases, you will discover that you really don't want to change the main picture, just some minor details. You want the children, and you want to raise them; there are just some minor details (such as coping with the laundry) that are bothering you. This helps put things into perspective.

Another fact to keep in mind is that adults enjoy other adult company, and no matter how cute a baby may be, he cannot supply adult conversation or mental stimulation. A young mother may need to talk to other adults during the day. Perhaps she should find a *shiur* or mother's group to attend. If she does not wish to leave the house, she can listen to a Torah tape or read a book of Jewish content. A mother who gives her attention to her children, and spends her time thinking about them will realize that motherhood is a very creative job.

A wife should be careful not to project her frustration onto her husband. It is not his fault. Of course he should make every effort to understand the situation, but it is difficult for someone to understand the feelings of another unless he has actually experienced those feelings at some time or other.

> Rachel is home all day with six-month-old Meira. Meira is a demanding child and Rachel feels quite frustrated by the end of the day. The minute Shalom arrives home from work, she hands him the baby. "Here," she says, "I had her all day, now it's your turn. I have to get out a bit." How do you think Shalom feels? Why can't Rachel arrange for a babysitter to come for an hour a day so that she can be refreshed and pleasant toward Shalom when he arrives?

If a babysitter is not feasible due to economic or other considerations, Rachel should think of other possible solutions to this problem. Perhaps she can arrange with a friend to watch her child for a short while and her friend will reciprocate by watching Meira another time. If Meira does indeed nap during the day, Rachel might use that time to rest so that she can be in a proper frame of mind to relate to Shalom pleasantly.

Baila has three small children. A friend offered her a ride to the shopping mall at four o'clock. She was about to go and then she thought, "I will come home at half past five, hot and tired. My children will be hot and tired. My husband will come home soon after that, hungry, hot and tired. Dinner will not be on the table. Everyone will get on each other's nerves. It isn't worth it. I will go shopping earlier tomorrow and maintain my *shalom bayis*."

**Message 41:** I will try to make the necessary arrangements to maintain *shalom bayis* when our home is blessed with children.

◆ Creating a calm environment

A woman often sets the tone and atmosphere of the home. Usually more can be accomplished in a calm atmosphere than in a tense one. If you make a conscious effort to present a pleasant demeanor, even if you are tense inside, you will help other members of the household remain calm. If there are twelve things left to do and there is only one hour left until Shabbos, you have more of a chance of getting them all done if you move smoothly and quickly from one job to another than if you run around in a frenzy. If assistance is available, you can enlist it by calmly assigning tasks in an organized manner. Imagine that you are being recorded on videotape, and think how you must look to your husband. Clearly, a calm demeanor is advantageous in promoting *shalom bayis*. [In some cases, the husband is more even-tempered than the wife, and the wife can try to emulate her husband in this matter.]

I met my friend Becky at a wedding. I knew that she had recently given birth, so I offered my *mazal tov*. In the course of conversation, Becky explained to me that all was not exactly well. "The baby needs a lot of medical attention," she said. She proceeded to explain to me what was wrong and that orthopedic surgery would be needed. "But the way I look at it," she continued, "is that everyone gets tested in life, and I am thankful that I was given something that is correctable." I asked her how her husband was faring, and she said that she had made a conscious decision to cope and this had a calming effect on her husband and family.

I find this story particularly heartwarming since the stress of an illness in the family can often contribute to tension between the husband and wife. Becky wisely set the home atmosphere so that the family willingly joined together to face the challenge. If she and her husband had felt inner turmoil and were not able to discuss it, they might have vented their frustrations at each other.

Message 42:  Are we creating a calm atmosphere in our home?

The ability to cope can make our lives much more pleasant. Difficult situations arise and a positive attitude is very helpful. We should always pray for the strength to deal with whatever difficulties arise. If a poor person asks for a donation, he wishes a donation, not a lecture on how he should trust in Hashem to provide for his needs. Similarly, if someone is under stress, he does not want a lecture on how he shouldn't let stress affect him; he wants and deserves empathy and acceptance. Afterward, hopefully the person can be shown how to cope, either by example or through suggestions. Recommendations are more readily received if the person realizes that they are being given out of a genuine desire to make his life more pleasant.

## Chapter Nine
## Money

A recent study showed that money was the main cause of quarreling in a marriage. I would list many causes ahead of money (lack of respect for one's spouse would probably head the list), but I have to agree that money can cause difficulties. This is due to several factors. Money is a necessity. Often there is not enough for basics, like food, and there is almost never enough to buy everything that one wishes. In addition, men often feel that it is their responsibility to support their families, and their sense of self-esteem is affected by their ability to provide.

◆ Shared money

The main way to avoid money problems in a marriage is to view all money as "our" money. It does not matter if it was brought in through the husband's paycheck or the wife's paycheck, or given as a gift by a relative of either spouse. Once it has entered the household, it is shared money. Both spouses together make intelligent decisions about how the money should be spent, and do not engage in me versus you-type arguments. Discussions about money should always reflect a "we" approach. The situation will be even more palatable if the couple can view the amount of money they have as the amount that Hashem has decreed they should have for that year.

> Leeba would like to eat out once a week. She reminds Meir that many of their friends frequently eat in restaurants. (Avoid comparisons, Leeba.) Meir points out that this is not an expense that they can afford, and food is just as nutritious and tasty if it is eaten at home. Leeba is upset and, in her anger, blames Meir: "If you had a better job, we could afford to eat out." Imagine Meir's feelings! He already secretly feels terrible that he is not earning more money. He wishes that he could support his family in royal style. Now he finds that his wife does not appreciate how hard he works, and his feelings of inadequacy are growing. He may answer back with some biting comment, putting down Leeba. This whole incident could be avoided if Leeba would recognize that Meir's opinion is a realistic assessment, and that eating out is not in the budget right now. Alternately, if Leeba feels they are "impoverished," they could discuss the situation as "we" and work out an affordable compromise. Perhaps they could eat out once every three months as a special occasion.

Message 43: I have to be careful not to let money cause conflicts.

### ◆ A realistic budget

A budget is very useful to a couple in assessing how much money is available. Some couples may feel comfortable with a detailed budget, while others feel more comfortable with a generalized budget. In either case it is very important not to fall into the bad habit of spending more than one has. Although frugal spending is important, it is difficult and uncomfortable to live with the constant pressure of "but we can't afford this, we can't afford that." One family I know was so strict that they did not go to a *simchah* because a present was not in their budget. A vacation was in their budget, so they did go on vacation. Spending should be within reason and with reason (*sechel*). Sometimes there may be extenuating circumstances and a loan will be called for. People should realize that a loan comes along with the responsibility to make arrangements for repayment.

In many cases a wife works to supplement the family income. This is a decision that should be arrived at after careful consideration. The husband and wife should discuss all the angles of the situation before deciding whether she should work outside the home. The options of working full time, part time, or not at all, should all be explored. The decision should be reevaluated after some time to see if the circumstances have changed. If there are children, their needs must be taken into account. Sometimes a woman feels that she must work, but it proves detrimental to the family. Often, the advice of a *Rav* or wise outsider can be helpful before making a decision about whether or not a wife will work.

> Rachel was a teacher on maternity leave after the birth of her second child. She had assumed that she would be going back to work, and she knew the income would be helpful. However, Rachel saw that she was not recovering as well as she had hoped to, and she did not feel up to returning to work.
>
> She and her husband discussed the situation, and they decided that Rachel's health was more important than the income. Rachel was very gratified that her husband was supportive, and that he was willing to make adjustments in the family budget to accommodate the reduced income.

**Message 44: A well-thought-out, flexible budget is helpful.**

◆ The "we must have it" syndrome

Money does not buy happiness. Money can buy goods and services that make life easier and more enjoyable, but the desire for more and more "things" can make life less enjoyable. Before deciding to make a purchase, it is helpful to evaluate whether the purchase is a necessity or a luxury. Is it a luxury that will make life easier and better? Is it something that we both agree on? If a woman wants something that her husband opposes, she would be wise to decide whether this is an item that she wants so much that she would be willing to jeopardize her *shalom bayis* for it.

Some people mistakenly believe that husbands who truly care about their wives buy them whatever they want. This is not true, and the husband may be motivated by a realistic approach to the budget and feel that this purchase is not warranted. The situation might be reversed, with the husband making impulse purchases and the wife viewing the situation realistically. In all cases, a balance must be achieved between the amount of necessities and luxuries you purchase. The focus should be on "us" deciding whether to buy something, not one spouse versus the other.

> Finances were tight in the Weiss household. Feivel made it clear to Shaina that she should limit her purchases. Shaina was trying her best, but one day she just couldn't resist a few items — all on sale — and before she knew it she had spent over $100. How will Feivel react? Does he realize that the purpose of money is to maintain a household, and will he be careful not to let money become a source of contention? Hopefully he can view the matter as Feivel and Shaina facing the purchases and not Feivel against Shaina.

A different story:

> Finances were tight in the Weiss household. Feivel made it clear to Shaina that she should limit her purchases. Shaina was trying her best to comply. One day Feivel arrived home with a large bag and a smile on his face. The local toy store was having a sale, so he bought each of the children a little toy. Shaina was frustrated and hurt. Had

Feivel been making her life difficult, when in fact there was money to be spent as long as he was doing the spending? Hopefully, Shaina will realize that Feivel did not make the "no buying rule" in order to make her life miserable. It was necessary. And what about Feivel's little shopping spree? Well, no one is perfect, and his fault was that he got in the mood to bring the children a treat. Budget had come in second to fatherly love. If Shaina accepts Feivel's choice, hopefully he will accept when she makes a similar choice.

**Message 45: Purchases should be viewed in their proper perspective.**

◆ Keeping up with the Cohens

The danger of making comparisons between people has already been pointed out (chapter 1). Similarly, looking at other families and wishing that you could live on their standard is also dangerous. A wife might direct her frustration at her husband when she is not able to acquire what her friends have. Again, if the money can be viewed as "our" money, given to us by Hashem, this problem can be solved.

> The Schwartzes just had an addition built onto their house. Is that going to be a source of tension for me?

> The Golds took their whole family to Disneyland for a week. Does my family therefore "deserve" to go?

> A bar mitzvah is coming up in the family. Will it be as fancy as the Shapiro's?

The list of luxuries that become necessities grows and grows. The more people see what others have, the more they want and the less happy they become. Extreme care must be taken to avoid the trap of trying to keep up with the standards of others.

**Message 46: I will try to concentrate on what I need, not on what others have.**

No discussion of money would be complete without the mention of *tzedakah*. Early in a marriage a couple should incorporate *tzedakah* into their budget, and both husband and wife should always work together to perform this important mitzvah. It is a mistake to assume that short-changing *tzedakah* will help in a tight financial situation; the best way to assure financial success is to give *tzedakah*.

When setting up *tzedakah* guidelines, *she'elos* should often be asked. Clarification is necessary regarding the amount to give, as well as priorities in *tzedakah*. Which types of needs should receive priority and where the money should be channeled are both topics that can be discussed with a *Rav*. A couple that approaches finances with an attitude of togetherness and Torah guidance will avoid monetary strife and enhance *shalom bayis*.

# Chapter Ten
## Anger — Part One

At this point in the book, a *kallah* may be saying to herself, "I certainly hope that my marriage will not be like those in the stories here. I am marrying someone whom I care deeply about, and I do not anticipate constant squabbles and arguments. Why can't I hear stories of fulfillment and love?"

In truth, engaged couples should feel optimistic and positive. Many couples have smooth, near-perfect relationships, and do not need to hear about anger control or other corrective measures. The joy felt by the engaged couple becomes deeper and more meaningful as time goes on. Some couples will have slightly imperfect times that are infrequent and short-lived. The goal of this book is to present examples of these possible pitfalls, along with methods to deal with them. Therefore, please read these chapters on anger with this in mind. Hopefully, you will need this information only infrequently, but this information can be helpful at some point.

Much has been written about the negative character trait, anger. Anger control is a worthwhile goal everyone should strive for. Ideally, each *chasan* and *kallah* concentrates on self-improvement before they get married to such an extent that no negative *middos* (character traits) enter or hinder the marriage. Practically, since we are all imperfect people who have not yet completed our process of character perfection, we will, upon occasion, react with anger. Some people are more prone to anger than others, and some people have been more successful than others in controlling it.

In reality, most married people occasionally feel and show anger toward their beloved spouses. Anger is destructive to a relationship and techniques must be learned to assure that relationships are not damaged in anger. This chapter and the following one will both discuss anger. This chapter will concentrate on control of anger. The next chapter will discuss one's reaction to the anger of another.

Is anger ever appropriate? Acting angry is sometimes necessary as a teaching tool. A parent may have to show anger toward a child to emphasize that his action was unacceptable. Similarly, a teacher may demonstrate anger to prove a point. In either of the above cases, the teacher or parent is more capable of proving the point if he or she is showing anger, but not feeling anger. When one feels anger, it is more difficult to teach effectively. Righteous anger is sometimes proper when facing a violation of *halachah*. However, each person should ascertain whether or not he has any personal involvement in what happened, because the anger might have been caused by a personal affront, and not by the injustice of the situation. In the vast majority of instances, anger is an inappropriate reaction.

◆ Acknowledging anger

"I'm not angry!" the angry person frequently maintains. The first step in anger control is to acknowledge that one is angry. Anger is a natural reaction to certain circumstances or a certain action. A *kallah* would be amazed to hear which insignificant events can spur anger toward those we love best. In many instances, anger results when a person's pride has been damaged.

After admitting anger, the next step is to dissipate it. Dissipating anger is not the same as burying or swallowing it. When anger is swallowed, it sits under the surface and eventually erupts. It is similar to an earthquake where the pressure eventually breaks through the ground. How can anger be dissipated? The proper technique is to talk to oneself and think of ways to calm down.

> Shaul was detained at work and he didn't call to inform his wife, Shuli. Dinner burned and Shuli was very upset. She could let her anger build, or she could try to dissipate it. If she does not consciously attempt to dissipate her anger, here is how the story might end:
>
> Shuli kept alternating her glance between the burned chicken and the clock. "Oh that Shaul, late again. And he doesn't even have the decency to call. He doesn't care about my feelings. Doesn't he realize that I worry about him? I'm always considerate of his feelings..."
>
> By the time Shaul comes home, Shuli cannot restrain herself. "Late again, huh? Why don't you ever have the consideration to call me?"
>
> Shaul's thoughtlessness stemmed from forgetfulness: he did not deliberately decide not to call. How will he feel after hearing this outburst?
>
> If Shuli does try to dissipate her anger, she will say to herself, "Wow, I'm really angry at Shaul. Looking at it from my point of view, he has really wronged me. But let me find ways to calm myself. Okay, he slipped this time, but I'm sure that I also have been inconsiderate in the past. He probably became involved with things and didn't realize I was waiting for him, or maybe he was unable to phone. If this is the worst he does, I guess I'm pretty lucky. I will keep telling myself that he didn't mean to hurt me, and think of the good things he has done."
>
> If Shuli keeps talking to herself, by the time Shaul comes home she will probably be calm enough to say, "Oh, welcome home. Dinner is ready. Sorry it's a little

overdone, but I thought you'd be home earlier. I'd really appreciate if you'd call me when you are going to be late, so I'll be able to plan better."

Message 47: After I accept my feelings of anger, I will try to dissipate them.

### ◆ Silent anger

Shuli had an advantage, since she had a few minutes to calm down before Shaul came home. One of the most important rules pertaining to anger is to try to remain silent while angry. The influence of anger is similar to the influence of alcohol. Unintended words leave the mouth unwittingly and much damage can be done.

Every person should make the commitment in an introspective moment not to speak while angry. It is very important to make this commitment in advance because, when people are angry, they want to speak and they want to say hurtful remarks.

Civilized people control their hands and do not resort to physical abuse, but they feel justified hurling words and engaging in verbal abuse. Sometimes a person controls his verbal response, but conveys the same angry messages in nonverbal gestures. These too should be avoided.

It is often advantageous to leave the room when angry, since it is difficult to remain silent in the presence of those whom you are angry at. Leaving the room may be seen as an offensive behavior, but it is definitely preferable to staying and speaking while angry. An apology in advance can also be very beneficial.

Elisheva knows that she has a temper, but she is surprised that she recently has been getting angry at Aryeh, her wonderful, helpful husband. One evening, while Elisheva and Aryeh are out walking, Elisheva swallows her pride and tells Aryeh, "I find myself getting angry lately. I don't know what it is. I guess that I am under too much pressure. Please understand that it is not your fault; it's my problem. If I get angry, I will leave the house and take a walk. I feel that is the best way to make sure I don't say hurtful things."

**Message 48: I will try my best not to speak while angry.**

◆ Methods of calming down

When you get angry, the goal is to leave your state of anger behind as quickly as possible. There are many ways to facilitate this.[*] One of the well-known methods of calming down is to count silently until the anger abates. One *Rav* had a special coat that he put on when he was angry. The act of putting on the coat gave him time to reflect on his anger.

Another method of calming down is to talk to yourself about your anger and its causes. "I know that I am angry now and I think that I have the right to be angry. But let me ask myself a few questions:

> If this same incident happened in another family, would I consider it something that another wife should get angry about?

> If someone else, other than my husband, did this to me, would I be angry at that other person?

> Is this big enough for me to waste my energy getting angry about?

> Is this something that I will remember next year or even next week?

> Would I feel so angry about this same incident if I were in a better mood?

---

[*] *Gateway to Happiness* by Rabbi Zelig Pliskin and *EMETT* by Miriam Adahan are two books on this topic.

Is there another explanation that I am not considering; am I giving the benefit of the doubt?

If I had done this thing, would I think that someone else had the right to get angry at me because of it?

If I had done this thing, would I excuse myself?

Is it possible that this wasn't done intentionally?

Hopefully, by the time you finish answering these questions honestly, the anger will subside.

Message 49: When I get angry, I will ask myself questions to examine how valid my anger is.

◆ Adjusting expectations

All people subconsciously accept certain things that they are powerless to change. Although rainy weather is frustrating when an outing is planned, it is futile to get angry at the weather. We cannot expect the weather always to be pleasant. Similarly, if both spouses accept certain behaviors in their partner, they will be less likely to become angry when those behaviors are exhibited.

If we expect someone to perform a certain way and he doesn't, we will feel upset that our expectations have not been met. If we do not have these expectations, we will not feel disappointed about them.

If a wife expects a husband to be sincerely concerned about how her day went, she will be annoyed every time he does not express a deep interest in her activities. If she lowers her expectations and does not assume that he should always inquire about her day, she will not be disappointed when he forgets to ask. This does not mean that things can never improve. A wife can politely tell her husband that she would appreciate it if he could take the time to listen to her tell about the events of her day, and hope that he improves.

> Nachmi never notices what Shoshi is wearing. It is frustrating and upsetting to Shoshi. She has fished for compliments and even pointed out her outfits to Nachmi, but all she gets is a vague "very nice." Shoshi can get angry every time she wears a new outfit, or she can lower her expectations and accept the fact that Nachmi doesn't pay attention to clothes.

> The light bulb is burned out in the closet. Penina has reminded Hillel several times that the bulb needs to be changed. Hillel has agreed to do it, but he hasn't gotten around to it. Every time Penina enters the dark closet she grows angrier and angrier. Although Penina is justifiably annoyed that the bulb has not been changed, anger is not productive. First, Penina should remind Hillel in a pleasant tone of voice. Perhaps he forgot about it, and Penina will not accomplish anything by waiting silently. If Penina can accept that for some reason Hillel is not going to change the bulb, and she changes it herself, then all the destructive feelings can be avoided.

Needless to say, certain things should be expected, and they cannot be overlooked. If Hillel was procrastinating about building the *sukkah* instead of changing the light bulb, Penina would have to deal with the situation differently. Anger is still not the proper way to get the *sukkah* built. If Penina explodes at Hillel about how lazy he is and that their family will be the only family without a *sukkah*, the *sukkah* probably will be completed, but the positive relationship between Hillel and Penina will be affected in the process. Penina has to be clever enough to think of some constructive way to motivate Hillel to act. If she is under the influence of anger, this will be much more difficult to do.

Message 50: I will try to accept those things that I cannot change, as well as those that are not worth the effort and aggravation to change.

### ◆ Changing anger to pity

Another technique which can be effective in reducing anger is to change it to pity. Rather than feeling angry at someone for an action, one can instead feel sorry for the person who acted in such an inappropriate manner. Pity is not a destructive emotion. However, the person should not be aware that you pity him, since most people do not like to be pitied. A person who is motivated by compassion will more effectively help another improve than a person who is angry.

I taught this concept of replacing anger with pity to a class of teenage girls. They listened attentively, but I was unsure how much they had internalized. The very next day an incident occurred which proved that indeed they had been listening and absorbing well. It was the day of the annual Science Fair, and the girls displayed their projects which were the results of weeks of work.

The science teacher came into class with a very serious look on her face. "I don't know how to tell you this, girls, but some of the younger children ran through the display and damaged several of your projects. You have a right to be very angry about this."

My students responded, "We are not angry at the children; we feel sorry for them that they haven't yet learned to respect other people's property." The science teacher was truly impressed and probably quite puzzled by the mature attitude of the teenagers. When they proudly reported the incident to me the next day I was gratified to see that my lesson had been put into practice so quickly, and I hoped that the lesson would stay with the girls for many more years to come.

**Message 51:** I will try to redirect my feelings from anger to pity whenever possible.

### ◆ Resentment

Resentment is similar to anger. People become upset and resentful when they feel that they have been wronged. Often, resentment is directed at a husband when something isn't his fault. People tend to take out their resentment on those closest to them, perhaps because they feel that they will be accepted despite their remarks. If a wife is tired and overworked, she may resent that her husband does not have similar obligations. If a baby wakes up several times in the middle of the night, it is frustrating, and a mother may become resentful. She cannot take out her resentment on her little innocent infant, so she may make the mistake of directing it at her husband.

Resentment, like anger, can be analyzed and dissipated. The main key to control of both anger and resentment is *dissipation.* When anger or resentment is dissipated, it is acknowledged, confronted, and dispelled until a calm demeanor returns.

There are many techniques to dissipate anger, and only several of them have been discussed in this chapter. Because anger is such a widespread problem, it is beneficial to read additional works on the topic (see p. 75).

*Chapter Eleven*
*Anger — Part Two*

It is difficult to deal with personal feelings of anger. It is even more difficult to deal with another person's anger when it is directed at you. When someone is angry at you, you can feel hurt and unloved. Your self-image can plummet as a result of angry confrontations. If no one ever got angry, then no one would ever be the recipient of anger. However, in our world of imperfect people, some will get angry, and others have to listen when it is expressed.

How can this situation be dealt with? If everyone would internalize the messages of the previous chapter, this chapter would be unnecessary. But as long as there are people who cannot control their tempers, those who are the targets of such people have to be given the tools to deal with their lapses.

Although the recommendations in this chapter advocate silence in the face of anger, let it not be thought that a wife should allow herself to suffer angry outbursts on an ongoing basis without any recourse. In many cases the wife can communicate her displeasure to her husband and he will reevaluate his angry reactions. In other cases the couple can discuss what circumstances lead to an angry reaction (such as tension or overtiredness), and the causes can be mitigated. Often the husband needs to be reminded of the importance of restraint when speaking to his partner in life. A wise advisor can bring this point home.

However, while someone is angry, he is often unable to listen to reason. At the time of the anger, a wife needs to be given tools to be able to ride out the outburst without exacerbating the situation. Her ability to rise to the challenge and ignore his angry comments is enhanced if she realizes that one's peace of mind is more dependent on how one reacts to a situation than on the situation itself. The wife can minimize her agitation and in turn her reactions by opening her "mental umbrella" (see below). If she can muster the emotional strength to maintain her equanimity in this difficult challenge, then she is truly the winner. Her mature attitude will eventually lead to greater *shalom bayis*.

#### ◆ A mental umbrella

If you are subjected to an angry tirade, the first thing to do is to open your "mental umbrella." This umbrella will function as a barrier, and those angry words will not rain down upon you. You can shield yourself from the words with several mental messages. First, you can remind yourself that saying something in anger is like saying it in a drunken stupor. After a person has let himself fall into the clutches of his own anger, he is barely in control of what he says. It is very difficult to deal with hurtful comments made by one spouse to another while in a state of anger. Those comments should be canceled; they were not intended.

But if he said it he meant it, one might think. Wrong! People under the influence of anger say many things they do not mean. If a husband says, "You are the most ungrateful person in the world," do you think that he has systematically evaluated everyone else's behavior and come to the conclusion that his wife is the most ungrateful person in the whole wide world? Of course not! He just wanted to vent some of his anger and deal a verbal blow.

> Bina and Dov were traveling. They made a wrong turn and traveled a long distance in the wrong direction. When Dov realized the mistake, he was hot, tired, and very angry. Of course he should have calmed himself down with the techniques discussed in the previous chapter, but he didn't. Instead he vented his frustration on Bina. "Why didn't you get the right directions?" he yelled. "I can't leave anything for you to take care of."
>
> Bina silently opened her mental umbrella and told herself, "Right now Dov is under the influence of anger. He's going to say things that he doesn't mean and he'll blame me for the mixup. I know that he is just as much at fault as I am, and he will soon calm down." So, she sits quietly and does not say anything, feeling secure that her worth as a person has gone up and not down by her mature behavior. After a cold drink, Dov begins to return to himself.

Message 52: I will open my mental umbrella when necessary.

◆ Problem de-escalation

If someone is spoken to in anger, an automatic reaction might be to answer back. The popular notion is that one is entitled to stand up for his rights and not allow another to take advantage of him. However, by one's contributing to the discussion at a time of anger, the dispute will escalate. Each verbal blow will be met by another blow, and a full-scale fight will erupt. On the other hand, if one can accept the tirade in silence, it will die down sooner. People have the option of pouring gasoline on a fire or pouring water on it. (It is interesting to note that our daily *tefillos* include a request for the strength to remain silent in the face of negative comments.)

There are two reasons why it is difficult to remain silent. First of all, people wish to present the facts as they perceive them. Second, since it is frustrating to the angry person when his verbal attacks are met with silence and a sense of calm, he may try to taunt the other person into an emotional response. But there is one overriding reason why it is better to keep quiet — the episode will pass more quickly if this rule is adhered to. There is basically not much of a future for a one-sided fight.

> One *Rebbe* used to give out little flasks of water to people who came to complain about their marriage quarrels. "Take this holy water," said the *Rebbe*, "and when your husband begins to raise his voice, put it in your mouth. Do not swallow it. It is guaranteed to make him stop more quickly." (In reality, the *Rebbe* was helping the wife to keep quiet.)

**Message 53: If I don't answer back, the anger will pass more quickly.**

◆ Listen and plan

Even if words are spoken in anger, they should not be totally discarded. There may be a valid message that should be heard. If this message is ignored, then anger about it might return. In addition, people do not like to feel that they are being ignored. A good approach is to say, "Thank you for bringing this to my attention. I'll take it under advisement."

A wise wife can also try to plan so that her husband will not get angry. If there are situations that annoy him, with proper foresight, they can often be avoided.

> Pinchas enjoys sitting down to a quiet, uninterrupted dinner. Chavi enjoys talking on the phone, and often ends up talking during supper. Pinchas doesn't realize that he needs a calm supper during which he and Chavi can discuss the day's activities. He also doesn't realize that he feels slighted when Chavi pays attention to the person on the telephone and not to him. One hour after supper Pinchas is in a bad mood and has indigestion.

If Pinchas realized the cause of his problem, he could verbalize it to Chavi before dinner time. "Chavi, I'd really appreciate it if you could ignore the phone during supper. I enjoy talking to you, and not eating alone while you talk on the phone." Or maybe Pinchas realizes the cause of the problem, but he doesn't tell Chavi because he doesn't want to appear demanding. (This is a miscalculation; speaking up in advance would definitely be better than anger afterward.) Maybe he is waiting for Chavi to realize the rudeness of her actions on her own. In any case, if Chavi gives some honest thought to the situation, hopefully she will realize the cause of the problem, and resolve not to answer the phone during supper.

> Message 54: I will try to avoid behaviors that cause anger.

### ◆ A philosophical approach

Everyone experiences some degree of discomfort in this world. If we realized how much discomfort we were being saved thereby in the World to Come, we would welcome the little tribulations that we endure. We cannot choose the type of trouble that we would prefer, but if we had the choice, most of us would choose verbal abuse over physical illness and pain. If we can view an angry speech as decreed from Hashem, it is less difficult to accept. If an adverse circumstance is labeled as a test, it is easier to withstand. Of course, no one should ever take it upon himself to be a messenger to deliver such discomfort, and it is lamentable if spouses end up causing unpleasantness to each other.

> Message 55: If I have trouble, it is ordained from Above.

### ◆ Thank God things aren't worse

There is a positive side to everything. If someone loses his temper once a month, thank Hashem that it isn't once a week. If it is once a week, thank Hashem that it isn't once a day. It is helpful to remember that many people have not yet perfected their character, and anger is a common human failing. At the same time you can pray that matters improve.

Hopefully, if the husband has a wife who knows how to calm things down, they very quickly will.

> Mr. Cohen suffered from a neurological disorder that affected his temperament. "I fly off the handle for just about no reason at all," the husband explained. "It is hard for me to live with myself. It must be impossible for my wife to live with me."
>
> "It sure is," proclaimed Mrs. Cohen. "But at least his anger is short-lived."

Message 56: I will try to focus on the positive and not on the anger.

It is my most fervent hope that no *chasan* or *kallah* ever has to be subjected to anger. However, since this is a problem that exists in marriages, it is important for a couple to establish rules. A wife can request that her husband not speak to her in anger. This may be a request that he cannot grant. Perhaps she can ask that he never speak to her in anger in front of others. Maybe she will request that he never discuss any of their disagreements with other members of the family. All these requests should be made when neither partner is angry at the other. When the anger passes, then a meaningful discussion can take place. In this discussion it is important that the husband and wife together try to resolve the problem of anger, without resorting to blame and personal affronts. Even if one spouse is capable of dealing with an angry outburst after internalizing the messages of this chapter, that should never be viewed as license for the other spouse to erupt.

If a husband or wife is often subjected to anger or other abusive behaviors, then help should be sought. Hopefully a couple can work together to overcome all challenges that arise in their marriage, including anger.

# Chapter Twelve
## The Berachah of Forgetfulness

The ability to remember is generally very helpful and important. However, in a relationship, sometimes the ability to forget is even more important. Those who can leave the past behind and face the future will save themselves needless aggravation.

◆ Forgive your husband as yourself

There is a prayer said before the nighttime *Shema* in which we forgive anyone who has wronged us. Whenever the spouse may have done something improper, it is especially important to forgive him as soon as possible. It is sometimes very difficult to swallow one's pride and to forgive, but the rewards are worthwhile. When people withhold forgiveness, they are stifling their relationships. It is easier to forgive someone who comes to apologize sincerely, but some people find it very hard to apologize, and they need to be forgiven nonetheless. We all would appreciate being forgiven for a misdeed before we plead for forgiveness. If an apology is offered, it should be accepted and its sincerity should not be questioned.

A wife can try to think of reasons to explain her husband's imperfect behavior. She should remember that she and her husband are both on the same side. "He's tired." "He's under a lot of pressure." "He meant to do the right thing." Once something is forgiven, it should also be forgotten. The slate should be clean again.

Hashem relates to us the way we relate to others. Do we not want Hashem to forgive us our past misdeeds? If we want Hashem to behave kindly toward us, it is incumbent upon us to work at acting kindly toward others.

> Chaya has been married for several years. One day she mentioned to her husband, Yona, "I remember that when we were engaged you wouldn't come with me to my friend's wedding."

Many days have passed since that incident, and hopefully Chaya's husband has done some good things since then. If Chaya, or any wife, is upset about something and cannot forget it, it is acceptable for her to mention the matter to her husband in a calm manner, and to give him the opportunity to apologize or explain the situation. Yona may explain that he had a headache that day. Perhaps he will confess that he didn't realize how much his company meant to Chaya, and if he had, he certainly would have come. Even if Yona has no valid explanation about why he was unavailable, the discussion will help Chaya realize that this is a relatively minor issue and she will get past it.

Message 57: I will try to forgive and not to bear old grudges.

◆ Apologize when necessary

You will be forgiving toward your husband and you hope that he will be forgiving toward you. You can assist him in his efforts to forgive by apologizing when appropriate, rather than justifying your actions. A simple, sincere apology can be very effective.

The heating bill came in the mail. Ettel put it aside in a good place and intended to give it to her husband, David. She inadvertently forgot, and the bill was now overdue.

"I'm sorry," said Ettel. "It was an oversight." Ettel chose an apology rather than a justification of her actions, and David forgave her right away. If she had said, "Here's the bill. Yes, I know it's late, but you also misplace things," then David would have been less likely to forgive.

**Message 58: An apology can be very beneficial.**

◆ Rewrite the script

You can make the past disappear from your memory, as if it never existed. When there is an episode that you want to forget, apply the "circle and peel" technique. Imagine that your life is written out on stickers. In your mind, circle the incident that you wish to forget, and peel it off the book of your life. Mentally imagine yourself crumpling that sticker and throwing it away. After you have discarded the incident, do not think or speak about it again.

Menachem feels very embarrassed about his behavior while at his in-laws the other day. He knows that he has to apologize for calling Rena "irresponsible" in front of her mother. How could he have done such a thing? He knows that disputes should be kept at home, and he doesn't think that Rena is irresponsible. But the words were said, and the damage was done.

He hesitatingly broaches the subject. "Um, Rena, about the other day when we were at your parents... that comment I made..."

"Forget it, Menachem, it's okay. I've already erased the incident. I know that you didn't really mean it; it just came out."

Menachem is relieved to know that he has such a forgiving wife. "But, Menachem," Rena continues, "perhaps the next time you speak to my mother, you can say something that will make her realize that you do not think that I am irresponsible."

◆ Today is the first day of the rest of your marriage

After the past is forgiven and forgotten, it is easier to look to the future. Each day should be viewed as the beginning of the rest of your marriage. If a husband had been doing something incorrectly, and has resolved to correct it, his wife should give him the opportunity to show that he is serious about his resolve. Change is difficult and, if a wife belittles her husband's efforts, he is likely to give up and not attempt to change. A wife has to be supportive and accepting of her husband.

> Rachel Leah lied to her mother several times. Now every time Rachel Leah says something, her mother doubts the veracity of her statements. This is not a pleasant situation, and Rachel Leah begged her mother to trust her.
>
> "Do you promise from now on to tell only the truth?" asked her mother.
>
> "Oh, yes!" said Rachel Leah.
>
> If Rachel Leah's mother has reason to believe that she will keep her promise, she should forget the past and not question the truth of the next statement her daughter makes. If she says to herself, "Well, Rachel Leah lied in the past; why should I assume that things will be different now?" things will probably not improve.
>
> If the mother decides to trust her daughter (unless she hears her lie again), then the past can be put behind them, and trust can be reestablished.

As a *kallah*, it is difficult to imagine all the things that bother married people. Before you get married is the perfect time to make a commitment not to dwell on little problems, but always to look forward at the goals that bind the two of you.

A well-known *rosh yeshivah* published an article about *shalom bayis* in which he recounted the following story:

> The *rosh yeshivah* was teaching a class to *chasanim*, and he urged them to let the little things go by. The example that he used was of a tube of toothpaste. If one finds that his wife did something terrible, like squeezing the toothpaste from the middle instead of the end, he should ignore it and not get upset. This example was met with laughter and disbelief. How could anyone get upset at his wife for something like that? The *Rav* decided that he had overdone it in his search for an example of a triviality that might upset someone, and he deleted this example from his lesson the next time.
>
> Several years later, the *Rav* received an interesting phone call. One of the students from that original class called to discuss what had happened the day before. The student, now a married man, had woken up, gone into the bathroom and seen the tube of toothpaste that his wife had squeezed from the middle. He began to get angry at his wife. How could she do such a thing? All of a sudden he remembered that he had been one of the students who had laughed at the thought that someone could possibly get angry at such an insignificant detail. Instead of yelling at his wife, he began to laugh at himself.

One who makes a conscious decision in advance not to get upset at little things will be spared much aggravation. Many couples have fulfilling relationships and are not affected by these petty mishaps. If a couple is blessed with such a warm, giving relationship, this chapter is unnecessary. But even a couple who does experience minor setbacks can grow past them and achieve true happiness together by following the above recommendations.

## Chapter Thirteen
## Thoughts to Banish

There are certain thought patterns that are unproductive and detrimental to a marriage. I prefer not to mention negative thoughts; they are better left unsaid. However, I felt a need to enumerate some notions that occasionally come to mind in order to point out that these thoughts are not valid. If a negative thought comes to mind, the proper approach is to say quietly, "Right now this is how I think and feel. I will explain to myself what is wrong with this thought pattern until I no longer feel that way." A concrete example will clarify this method.

Shulamis feels that her husband, Mordechai, enjoys his friends' company more than hers. She has discussed the matter with him and he explained to her that this is not so. He does enjoy discussing old times with his friends, but he knows that a friend is not a wife, and nothing compares to the deep relationship between husband and wife. Shulamis now knows on an intellectual level that Mordechai chooses her far above his friends, but she still feels upset when he goes out with a friend.

She realizes that she must work on this feeling until she no longer feels this way. She begins to talk to herself. "Mordechai told me that he enjoys my company more than that of his friends. I have no reason to doubt it. I enjoy talking to my friends, and I have to keep telling myself that he is also permitted to spend time with his friends."

If she keeps talking to herself, she will work the bad feeling out of her system. On the other hand, if she says, "Well, this is how I feel. Mordechai is going to have to change his habits, because I can't help the way I feel," she will make life difficult for both of them.

Below is a list of thoughts that should be canceled if they come to mind.

◆ Thought to banish #1: "We will never disagree."

It is unreasonable to assume that two different people will always agree on everything. An argument does not signify a troubled marriage. It just signifies that two people are not in agreement on a specific issue. The goal is to disagree without being disagreeable. A wife may be convinced that her position is the correct one, but she has to be careful that she does not present it in a condescending manner. Many newly married couples feel terrible after their first disagreement. Don't blow it out of proportion. Just pass it by and move on.

◆ Thought to banish #2: "What am I getting out of this marriage?"

People enter marriage with unrealistic expectations of what it will do for them. They think that once they marry, they automatically will be happy and will be able to surmount their personal problems. When they realize that marriage has not changed them much, they may begin to wonder if this means that there is a problem with their marriage.

In the long run, a marriage relationship can be the catalyst for much growth on the part of both husband and wife, but it is wisest to replace the above question with another one. Rather than ask, "What am I getting out of this marriage?" each person should ask himself or herself,

"What am I giving to the marriage?" It is through giving that one eventually receives.

♦ Thought to banish #3: "Other husbands are much better than mine."

The danger of comparisons has been pointed out. It is impossible to compare people, and although it appears that another husband is better, reality may be very different than appearance. Your husband is truly the best — for you.

♦ Thought to banish #4: "If he loved me, he would act differently."

Many people look for signs of love and misinterpret actions as evidence of lack of love. "If he loved me, he would do this for me." "If he loved me, he wouldn't say that." "If he loved me, he would offer to help me more." In most cases, his behavior does not show a lack of love, but rather a different character trait. Perhaps a husband isn't helping because he doesn't know that his wife needs or wants help. Maybe his trait of helpfulness needs refining. If you hear yourself thinking, "If he loved me...," stop those thoughts and look for other explanations to the situation.

♦ Thought to banish #5: "He isn't trying to understand me."

It may appear that a husband is not making any effort to understand his wife. Most likely, he wishes that he could understand her, but he is baffled by the differences between male and female psychology. "I said a little joke, and she goes off crying?" Husbands do not automatically understand their wives. If you communicate your feelings clearly, perhaps one day your husband will succeed in understanding you. And if not, many marriages are happy even if the husband does not totally understand his wife.

◆ Thought to banish #6: "If he would behave more appropriately toward me, then I would behave more appropriately toward him."

It has already been pointed out that every husband and wife should be working independently to promote *shalom bayis*. It is much easier to be nice to someone who is nice to you, but the obligation is there even if the situation is not optimal. You should work on your side of things, and hope and pray that he does the same.

◆ Thought to banish #7: "Why isn't my husband more spiritual?"

In school and in *sefarim*, we have learned about ideal behavior and thought. A wife who expects her husband to live up to these ideals will be disappointed when she discovers that he is a mere mortal. The job of a wife is to be encouraging, but not to be his *mashgiach* (moral supervisor). If you have reached a certain level in your spiritual growth, do not look down on him if he hasn't perfected that same area. Chances are that he has perfected different areas.

◆ Thought to banish #8: Doubts concerning your choice of spouse.

Once you have made your choice, which is Heavenly guided, never doubt that choice. If your thoughts start wandering in the direction of, "What would have been if I had married someone else," stop those thoughts immediately. There is no room for "what ifs." You have married the person destined for you, and it is with this person that you are capable of building happiness.

◆ Thought to banish #9: Thoughts of drastic action.

Almost all problems that come up in a marriage do not require drastic measures. Once a drastic move is made, it is hard to back down and return to normal.

Gila's husband complained one day that the coffee that she made for him wasn't hot enough. "In that case," said Gila, "from now on you can make it yourself."

How can Gila back down from her statement and make coffee for her husband after she has cooled off? It is wiser not to announce or implement such a change.

One of the thoughts that should be banished from your mind, and needless to say never verbalized, is the possibility of your leaving. Marriage is a lifelong commitment, and such a thought is detrimental to the foundation of your marriage. If a couple is committed to building a relationship, it will eventually flourish.

I hesitate to tell the story of Baruch and Bracha, but I feel that their story must be told. (In this true story, as in all the other stories in this book, the names and some of the details have been changed. The names Baruch and Bracha were chosen to signify the blessings that this young couple had. Unfortunately it took them quite a while to recognize them.)

Baruch and Bracha had been married for several months. Things did not look nearly as rosy as they had before the wedding. "Did I really marry the right person?" thought Bracha (thought #8). "I'm not happy being married (thought #2); maybe I should get out of this relationship (thought #9). Maybe there is someone better out there that I can find (thought #3)."

Instead of turning for help, Baruch and Bracha made one mistake after another and their relationship eroded. Bracha was the one who finally left and went to live with her parents, but Baruch felt relieved. He also felt very sad to think that he would have to be an absentee father to his infant son.

The story does not end here. A wise advisor realized that Baruch and Bracha had not made the wrong choice when they got married; they made the wrong choice when they separated. Instead of walking out of the relationship, they should have been searching for ways to make their relationship grow. The *Rav* saw that the situation was not hopeless, and took the time and effort to meet with both Baruch and Bracha many times. He taught them how to communicate, how to avoid blame, how to deal with anger, and many other techniques necessary for a relationship.

When Baruch and Bracha reunited, they were both more mature and ready to make their marriage work. This time they realized that marriage is a lifelong commitment, and that results are not immediate. To their credit, they put the past behind them and worked together to build a beautiful *bayis ne'eman*.

Imagine a situation where two people are told to search for a hidden treasure in a certain room. The first person is told that there definitely is a treasure in that room, while the second one is told that there may or may not be something in that room. The second person will give up after a short time, while the first one will continue searching until he finds the treasure. This is analogous to a marriage. One who views marriage as a room that definitely holds a treasure within, waiting to be uncovered, will keep working and searching until he succeeds in finding that treasure.

# Chapter Fourteen
## Enjoying Life Together

In a marriage, each partner can enhance the life of the other. Two are better than one, and two who have grown to be a unit are indeed fortunate. God, in His infinite kindness, gives people many gifts to enjoy. There are material possessions, rewarding experiences, and intangible spiritual pleasures — all gifts from Above. After acknowledging and expressing appreciation for these gifts, we then are to enjoy that which Hashem has given. The enjoyment is much greater if it is shared. A husband and wife who share such experiences can share much joy.

◆ Joy of purpose

A soldier who is given an important mission proudly marches off to do his duty. One who is saddled with a chore that he doesn't want drags himself to do it. By looking at a person's demeanor it is often possible to perceive his attitude toward his mission in life. A husband and wife who are as two soldiers marching side by side and building a *bayis* can look upon their mission with pride.

> The Langs were newly married and were guests of the Newmans, who had been married for several years.

"I remember when I was at your stage in life," Mr. Newman commented. "We felt like we were playing house, and gradually, after several years, the enormity of it all sank in. We were not playing, we were truly building a Jewish household. It is like watching a play in which you are the stars of the show. Keep on acting with enthusiasm."

**Message 61: Am I an enthusiastic soldier carrying out my precious mission?**

◆ Joy of sharing

A married couple can look upon that which they have built together, and share the joy of joint accomplishments. These accomplishments can be small or great; the important thing is that they are shared achievements. The couple can also share the wealth of blessings that they have received jointly from Hashem. A milestone in the life of a child is a tremendous opportunity for shared happiness. Any mitzvah that the couple has done, as well as any personal growth, are also causes for celebration. The opportunities are endless.

**Message 62: Do we share happy feelings together?**

◆ Enjoying little things

One who rejoices only at major events in life misses out on many small pleasures. An engaged or newly married couple tends to find the smallest events in life to be full of fun. Opening a new bank account is an adventure, choosing a piece of furniture is a delight. One goal is to keep finding enjoyment in life's minor events throughout the years.

> Simcha has the knack of making any chore into an enjoyable experience. When he brings in the groceries from the car, he announces his arrival, "Delivery man at your

service, ma'am." As he puts each item away, he makes some witty comment about the label or the contents.

Although not everyone is a born comedian, an enthusiastic approach adds joy to many events.

The Morris family had just gotten on the highway. It was the beginning of their vacation. They were not pleased when the car stalled out and could not be started up again. The hour they spent in the dreary drizzle waiting for the tow truck could easily have been unpleasant. But Mrs. Morris decided that this time, too, could be enjoyed, and she set the atmosphere for the family to look upon this mishap as an adventure.

The family made a delightful picnic in their car; the food tasted just fine. They asked the police officer who stopped for them many questions. He was interesting and informative, and he demonstrated how his car computer operated. The whole episode passed quickly and pleasantly.

**Message 63: Do I take time to appreciate small events in life?**

◆ Making life more pleasant for your spouse

As mentioned previously, after you are married, you have the opportunity to make life more pleasant for your husband. Each spouse can endeavor to find ways to make the other have a more pleasant day. If you are in a store and find a small gadget that you think your husband would like, consider buying it just to make his life more enjoyable. Often a pleasant greeting is even more important than a gift.

David was having a difficult day at work. He took a lunch break and found a cheerful note from his wife. He began to smile and his whole mood changed. He was reminded that there was someone who cared about him, and that his home was his refuge from work.

**Message 64:** What else can I do to make my husband's life even more pleasant?

Some of the stories in this book have been negative — to point out behavior patterns that should be avoided. Let it not be thought that every couple has to experience these types of incidents on a regular basis. A large percent of the time, life continues without mishap and marriage does not have to be regarded as a "job." If both husband and wife are happy people, they will infuse their marriage with that happiness, and many problems will never arise. Happiness can be an elusive goal, but it is not beyond reach. A couple that approaches life with a real enthusiasm for living, combined with a high level of serenity, is headed toward a lifetime of happiness.

## Chapter Fifteen
## In Conclusion, Dear Kallah

Happiness is ahead of you. As you begin your life together with your *chasan*, think of it as if the two of you are charting a course through the sea of life. Together you can navigate toward making great accomplishments. Occasionally, you might find that your ship is veering slightly off course. Endeavor to redirect it immediately, before it drifts further off course. A minor correction is relatively simple, but if a situation continues uncorrected, it is more difficult to put things back on course later. The trip is long and eventful. Focus on your destination and do not be deterred by setbacks along the way.

The word "yet" is a powerful word that can help you keep your goals in mind. Perhaps you will notice that you have not yet succeeded in a certain area. This does not frustrate you because success may be on its way. Your husband may not have learned to be sensitive enough, yet. Hopefully, he will learn soon.

If you encounter difficult areas, think of them as challenges rather than problems. Hashem only provides challenges that one is capable of handling. You approach these difficult situations with the confidence that a solution is within your reach. Analyze the situation and you will be surprised at the creative solutions that can find.

As a *kallah*, you may feel somewhat nervous. This is quite common, since people often are nervous and apprehensive in new situations. I hope that this book does not contribute to your worries. I have endeavored to present you with the tools to help your marriage grow and to point out to you what are the proper priorities.

Although nervousness may be a natural emotion to feel before your wedding, you can try to calm yourself. Your life is ahead of you, and you have many wonderful things to look forward to together. It is not good for people to be alone. It is good for two people to find each other and build a beautiful marriage together. They can become a source of strength for each other and find true happiness and fulfillment together. You enter marriage with this joy on your horizon, and the tools to acquire it.

Throughout this book there have been many references to *tefillah*. While it is important to put in the effort to promote *shalom bayis*, it is comforting to know that Hashem assists us at all times. We should pray to Him for help. We can ask, among other things, for the wisdom to be able to deal with difficult situations and the ability to maintain a positive attitude. Married people can also pray that their relationship will grow and that their marriage will always remain strong. If you keep your goals in mind at all times and invest the effort in your marriage, God willing you will be blessed with the happiness that you want. You will create a *bayis ne'eman* with a pleasant atmosphere, where children and their parents can grow and flourish.

I would like to conclude with a heartfelt *berachah* that *klal Yisrael* should have *nachas* from you and your *bayis ne'eman b'Yisrael.*